Equipoise: The Life and Work of

Alfredo Corvino

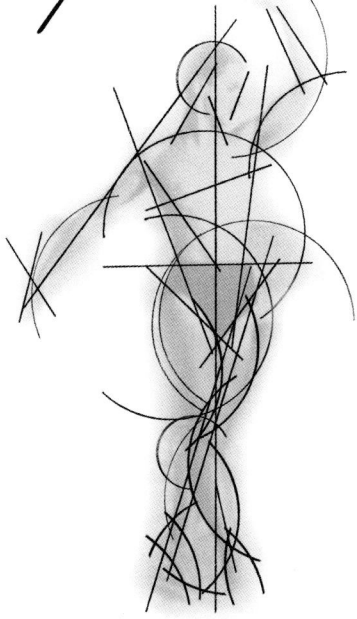

Dawn Lille

Dance & Movement Press™

New York

Published in 2010 by Rosen Book Works, LLC
29 East 21st Street, New York, NY 10010
Exclusively distributed by the Rosen Publishing Group, Inc., New York

Copyright © 2010 by Dawn Lille

First Edition

Editors: Nancy Allison, John Kemmerer, Abby Young, Karolena Bielecki
Book Design: Les Kanturek

Library of Congress Cataloging-in-Publication Data

Lille, Dawn.
Equipoise: the life and work of Alfredo Corvino / Dawn Lille.—1st ed.
    p. cm.
Includes index.
ISBN 978-1-4358-9124-1 (hard bound book)
1. Corvino, Alfredo, 1916–2005. 2. Ballet dancers—Uruguay—Montevideo—Biography.
3. Dance teachers—New York (State)—New York—Biography. 4. Ballet dancing—New
York (State)—New York—History. I. Title.
GV1785.C655L55 2010
792.802'8092—dc22
[B]
                                                    2009016948

Manufactured in Malaysia

CPSIA Compliance Information: Batch #TWW10YA: For Further Information contact Rosen Publishing, New York, New York at 1-800-237-9932

Front Cover: Alfredo Corvino, age twenty-two, April 12, 1938. Photographer
unknown. Photo courtesy of the Corvino archives.

Back Cover: Corvino at the entrance to the Folkwang School, Essen, Germany,
circa 1995. Photographer unknown. Photo courtesy of the Corvino archives.

To the Corvinos—Alfredo, Marcella, Andra, Ernesta

They knew and know that nothing is perfect, but with integrity and love almost anything is possible.

Contents

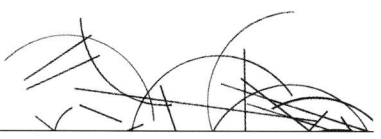

LIST OF ILLUSTRATIONS

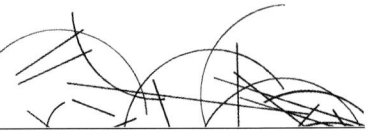

Early Photos (1800s–1961)

32. Corvino teaching at the current Juilliard Dance Division studios in Lincoln Center, New York City, 1976. *Photo © Peter Schaaf.*

33. The Dance Circle Company, New York City, 1978. *Photo by Les Carr. Photo courtesy of the Corvino archives.*

34. Fortieth anniversary celebration of the Juilliard Dance Division, New York City, 1992. *Photo by Stephanie Cimino. Photo courtesy of the Corvino archives.*

35. Corvino, the "whisper teacher," Paris, 1995. *Photo © Marion-Valentine. Photo courtesy of the Corvino archives.*

36. Corvino teaching company class for Tanztheater Wuppertal Pina Bausch, circa 2000. *Photo © Franceso Carbone.*

37. Corvino wearing the birthday gift from the Tanztheater Wuppertal dancers, 1999. *Photo by F. Suels. Photo courtesy of the Corvino archives.*

Six Photos Illustrating the Equipoise of the Corvino Approach to Classical Ballet Technique

38. Corvino in Léonide Massine's *Seventh Symphony*, circa 1941. *Photo © Maurice Seymour. Line drawings by Irene Dowd.*

39. Andra Corvino, studio portrait, 1970. *Photo by Les Carr. Photo courtesy of the Corvino archives. Line drawings by Irene Dowd.*

40. Ernesta Corvino as the Sleeper in her ballet *Somnus*, 1989. *Photo by Les Carr. Photo courtesy of the Corvino archives. Line drawings by Irene Dowd.*

41. Andra Corvino, studio portrait, 1981. *Photo by Les Carr. Photo courtesy of the Corvino archives. Line drawings by Irene Dowd.*

42. Andra Corvino as Mona Lisa in Ernesta Corvino's ballet *The Gallery*, 1981. *Photo by Les Carr. Photo courtesy of the Corvino archives. Line drawings by Irene Dowd.*

43. Ernesta Corvino as the Fifer in her ballet *The Gallery*, 1981. *Photo by Les Carr. Photo courtesy of the Corvino archives. Line drawings by Irene Dowd.*

FOREWORD

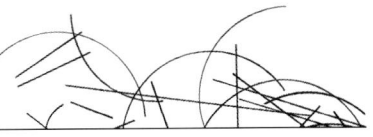

I suppose I have to get used to the idea . . .

There is no day that passes, no class I teach or take where I don't think of him. How could I not? No one could make you understand with such evidence and simplicity, the logic of the human body's mechanics. In other words how to function! The dynamics, the musicality of a movement—everything became so obvious, so organic in his classes! Do you know anybody who would press on his boxer's nose to make you realize you've got a sickled foot by doing a *tendu* in a certain way— and laugh about it? An unforgettable laugh.

It is as simple as this—I wouldn't still be dancing and enjoying it if I hadn't met him. For so many reasons . . .

Something I still haven't learned from him yet—how to travel with such a small suitcase, no matter where and for how long!

Thank you Maestro, Corvino, for still being with us!

Dominique Mercy
Tanztheater Wuppertal Pina Bausch
May 2009

ACKNOWLEDGMENTS

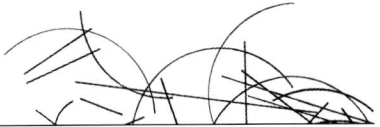

Without the sharing of memories, information, and time by the following, this book could not exist: Samir Akika, Nancy Alfaro, Richard Alston, Ahuva Anbury, Judith Chazin-Bennahum, Irene Clark, Margot Mink Colbert, Tina Curran, Gay DeLanghe, Mercedes Ellington, Alex Farkas, Toni Lacativa Farkas, Frederic Franklin, June Evans Goldberg, Ann Hutchinson Guest, Joyce Herring, Beth Hoge, Nancy Scattergood Jordon, Ellen Kogan, Rebecca Lazier, Carla Maxwell, Dominique Mercy, Janet Panetta, Stephen Pier, Anthony Salatino, Tonia Shimin, Peter Sparling, Richard L. Thomas, Lucy Venable, and Marguerite Wesley.

Jeni Dahmus, archivist, and Jane Gottlieb, head librarian, at the Juilliard School were patient, helpful, and of great assistance. John Pennino, archivist at the Metropolitan Opera, shared his materials. Madeleine Nichols and Pat Rader, at the Jerome Robbins Dance Collection of the New York Public Library for the Performing Arts at Lincoln Center, were always there in an emergency. Norton Owens, archivist at Jacob's Pillow, was his usual kind self. Suzanne Daone was a helpful backup on the computer. Rachelle Tsachor and Dalienne Majors, both former Juilliard students, were most generous in sharing the interviews they conducted with the Corvinos. I thank Carl Paris for rushing over to help with the translation of *Behind the Curtain* and Manuel de la Nuez for his help with the subtleties of the Spanish language and his support.

Nancy Allison, my editor and the person who suggested this undertaking, deserves a bouquet for her ideas and her patience.

The Corvinos—how fortunate I am, and richer, to have spent so much time with Marcella and Alfredo. Andra and Ernesta can never be thanked enough for their generosity and love.

"A dancer in first position is like a lit candle."

—Alfredo Corvino

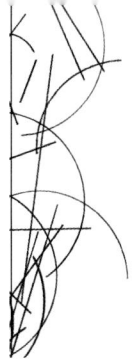

Chapter 1

CHILDHOOD AND
EARLY DANCE TRAINING

A lfredo Alfonso Corvino Jr. (nicknamed "Pocho," which means "pinchable") was born February 2, 1916, in Montevideo, Uruguay. He was the first child of Alfredo Alfonso Corvino and Doña Margarita Dolce. His father officially registered him on February 9, and that document indicates that the birth took place in his parents' home at Piedras 566, at 10:45 PM.

Corvino's father was twenty-eight years old, and his mother twenty. They lived on the second floor of a large house and always told the story of the melon seller coming by on the day of Pocho's birth. His mother purchased a large watermelon and went into labor after she carried it upstairs. Their son insisted, with his customary twinkle, that this was the reason he was especially fond of watermelon.

Margarita Dolce, called Julia, was the daughter of Francesco Dolce, born in Calabria, Italy, and Ernestina Villarino, an Uruguayan of Spanish descent. As a young man, Francesco had gone to Rome and had been employed there by the House of Savoy as a photographer, earning a cavalier medal from the government. He immigrated to Uruguay in 1874 and spotted the beautiful Ernestina on a tram in Montevideo. Together they would eventually have five children: Carlos, also a photographer; Chela, an artist; Humberto, who trained racehorses; Elena; and Julia. It is not known at what point Francesco revealed that he had seven illegitimate children, but the rest of the family all knew of their existence. According to his grandson Alfredo Jr., they even met some of them. Ever enigmatic, Corvino also said that everything in his grandfather's photography shop was held in the name of his brother, who was probably his business partner and evidently preceded him in death. What is known for certain is that after Francesco's brother died, his widow went off to Buenos Aires with all the money.

Suddenly impoverished, Francesco's other children now had to work for a living. Ernestina took Chela and Elena and went to live and work with Carlos, who was married by then and operating his own photography studio. Chela did the tinting of the photos, and Elena worked in the darkroom. Julia had been the first to get married. Her son remembered that at one point he lived in a large house with an extended family, including his grandmother, his aunt Elena, his aunt Chela, and Chela's husband and daughter.

Alfonso Corvino, Alfredo Jr.'s paternal grandfather, was a tailor from Avellino, a town one hour from Naples, Italy. He and his wife, Carmen Masseo, were part of a huge colony of Italians who had immigrated to Uruguay in the mid-nineteenth century, seeking a better life in the New World. Of their five children, Alfredo Jr.'s father was the baby and the only one born in Uruguay. When Alfredo Jr. was growing up, one of his uncles lived in the countryside. Another uncle, Graviel, owned one of the biggest cafes in Montevideo. His aunts— Concepción, who had five children, and Catalina, who had none—lived in Montevideo and were very successful.

Alfredo Sr. became a musician. He trained in Uruguay as a violinist and played in the Philharmonic Orchestra of Montevideo. He often worked days providing accompaniment for the silent films at the local movie theater and for musical revues that rolled into town. He was a very gentle, affectionate "ladies man." He was also a gambler, and these two tendencies would prove to be his downfall and a blight upon his family. How Alfredo Sr. met Julia Dolce, what their courtship was like, and how they came to be married was never discussed by the family.

A Difficult Childhood

From kindergarten until he was nine years old, Alfredo Jr. attended public school. He started to study the violin when he was seven because, as he put it, the instrument "was there waiting for me before I was born." Corvino claimed that he showed no real talent, and he believed his father was just as happy to have him abandon the instrument at age nine because he did not want his son to enter a profession in which he felt there was no future. Alfredo Jr. also studied voice. It is unclear whether or not he ever took formal classes in tap dance, but he said he used to tap backstage alongside those who auditioned for the musical revues in which his father played. When speaking about that time, Corvino implied that he watched these performers and then simply copied what they did. When they responded with encouragement, he kept going.

Young Alfredo began attending the Jesuit School at age ten and remained there until the age of twelve. There he remembered learning French (a language spoken by many in Montevideo at the time) and wearing a uniform of a white jacket and blue tie. Between his work with the symphony, the movie houses, and the musical revues that came to town, Alfredo Sr. was doing well, so the family could afford Pocho's private school tuition. But three years later, with the advent of the talkies, the worldwide Great Depression, and Alfredo Sr.'s increasing gambling debts, young Alfredo was forced to switch schools and enroll at Escuela España, a public school near Avenida Julia. Among other subjects, Alfredo Jr. studied carpentry and writing, in which he received honors. He quit school at age fifteen in order to help support his increasingly impoverished family.

The Corvino family became downwardly mobile, moving every couple of years, always to cheaper quarters. The large house his parents had rented and filled with family was soon replaced by an apartment on a small side street called Policia Viaja. This, in turn, was followed by a series of ever smaller and cheaper apartments as the family's financial situation worsened. Each move required Alfredo to make new friends, but he always had his cousins around him and the luxury of his own bedroom.

Young Alfredo landed his first job in 1931 as an office boy at an import/export firm called Heinz and Bonilla. His main objective was less to earn money than to learn how to type. Alfredo sometimes had trouble spelling correctly, and he thought typing would help him improve. His second job was in a municipal department of Montevideo where maps of the city were made. Corvino said he was quite successful in the design aspect of this trade, which is not surprising given the great sense of spatial awareness evident in his later dancing, choreography, and teaching.

Meanwhile, Alfredo Sr. had become so ill that he was unable to work much of the time. Within two years, he was dead from syphilis—a cause of death known to the entire family but never discussed by them. He was forty-four. Young Alfredo was only sixteen, and his sister, Margarita, was five.

Julia, now a widow, was tiny, bossy, feisty, and full of energy. She was also a very strict, devout Catholic and not prone to showy displays of love or maternal warmth. She tended to worry about everything, and this propensity probably caused her to seem distant as a parent. She had been a housewife before she was widowed, but upon her husband's death, she took a job in the narcotics division of the local police department, remaining there until her retirement.

The extended Corvino family had money at the time of Alfredo Sr.'s death, but it was never offered to Julia and her children. From the age of fifteen until his own death in 2005, Alfredo would contribute first to his mother's support and then his sister's. He bought them an apartment in Montevideo and set up a bank account for them that he constantly replenished with money from his own earnings. He met these self-assumed filial obligations without any sense of resentment or recrimination, although from an early age he would occasionally retreat into a solitary quietness.

An Early Love of Movement

It was while Alfredo was working in the cartography office that he started night school at the age of seventeen, but his return to academia would be cut short once again when he discovered dance. This discovery was a long time in the making.

One of the things that kept the young Alfredo positive and engaged—and that provided some much-needed continuity—throughout his somewhat tumultuous childhood was athletics. He shared this enthusiasm with his cousin and best friend, Humberto Dolce Jr., the son of his mother's brother. They were both members of the Athletic Union, where they participated in various sports. One day, they arrived at the union and saw a posting announcing an upcoming boxing competition that was Uruguay's equivalent of the Golden Gloves. Amateurs were encouraged to sign up for the competition. When Alfredo saw his name already written in, he asked, "Who put this here?" Humberto answered, "I signed up for this. If I do it, you have to do it, too."

Peer pressure prevailed over common sense and self-preservation. Alfredo entered the local competition, representing the Athletic Union, and surprisingly, he won. Furthermore, he went on to win the opportunity to represent his club in the national competition, but he came down with tonsillitis and had to pull out of the finals. His boxing category was flyweight, a class of boxing in which fighters must weigh between 108 and 112 pounds. He said he weighed in at about 106 pounds, which actually should have placed him in the light flyweight class. Although Alfredo Sr. never saw his son dance, he did see him box.

Another favorite sport of young Alfredo's was rowing, in which he also enjoyed great success. In fact, he won a local competition as both a single oarsman and as a double oarsman with Humberto. He also played a bit of basketball but was at a disadvantage due to his small stature. In track and field, Alfredo competed in short distance sprinting. He also started swimming in conjunction with his membership in the Rowing Club of Uruguay. Swimming was the only sport Alfredo continued to participate in once he started to take ballet classes.

The tale of how he first became interested and involved in dance is one that Alfredo Corvino told with great relish and a grin. His cousin Chela, known as "Chelita" to distinguish her from her mother (Julia's sister), was taking ballet lessons, and the entire family went to one of her recitals. Alfredo remembered that one piece was danced to one of the *Hungarian Rhapsodies* by Frank Liszt, and a harlequin figure appeared in another of the ballets. At the end of the performance, the family went backstage to talk to the dance teacher. Aunt Chela decided that her daughter would have a better chance of succeeding in ballet if she had some good male partners. She soon convinced her athletic nephews, Alfredo and Humberto, to audition for scholarships at the dance school. Because he was so short, his family really did not think Alfredo would be accepted. But the two "inseparables" did audition.

This time it was Alfredo who had to drag his reluctant cousin "into the ring." Humberto lasted for only two classes, but Alfredo's entire life was suddenly determined after his first exposure to dance at the age of seventeen. He spent the next two years working days at the mapmaking office and dancing nights, taking classes, rehearsing, and working on his own in the studio. This schedule forced him to discontinue night school, and he didn't receive a diploma until he was awarded an honorary doctorate from the Juilliard School in 2003.

An Important Mentor

Alberto Pouyanne (1899–1971), Alfredo Corvino's first and most influential teacher, was born in Montevideo into a wealthy family. He was only thirty-four years old when he met the young man who would become his most famous pupil. Pouyanne had demonstrated a talent for music at an early age and was sent to Paris to further his studies in piano. Once there, however, he became a dancer instead, hiding this news from his family for fear they would cut off their financial support. He studied with Gustave Ricaux, who had been a principal dancer with the Paris Opera Ballet; Jean Horain; Gala Chabelska, who had studied in Paris with Mathilda Kshessinska, the former *prima ballerina assoluta* of the Maryinsky Ballet; and Alexandre Volinine, who had trained and performed with the Bolshoi Ballet. Pouyanne performed in France, under a different name, with the Ballet de Romano, a small, relatively unknown company. He also gave a series of performances in France in which he both danced and played the piano.

In Paris, Pouyanne was exposed to the dance world's brightest luminaries. He had seen Isadora Duncan, the American dancer and iconoclast who danced barefoot and without corset and stressed the need for a completely expressive body, declaring that in her wildest dreams she could not envision the goddess of liberty dancing on *pointe*.

Pouyanne also became very familiar with the ballets of Michel Fokine, the Russian dancer, teacher, and choreographer whose approach to his art changed the history and direction of ballet in the twentieth century. Fokine's belief that the ballet dancer should be expressive, leaving technique in the classroom, echoed many of Duncan's precepts and made many of his ballet characters universal in nature.

Pouyanne returned to Montevideo in the early 1930s, ostensibly to teach music. Instead, however, he decided to teach ballet and began to choreograph. Elegant of stature and well educated, he seems to have been an intuitive, inspiring, and highly effective teacher. His school, the Academy of Ballet, was conveniently located across the street from the mapmaking division of the municipal office where Alfredo worked.

When Alfredo started taking ballet classes, Pouyanne at first taught him privately. Eventually, he took group classes and joined a small corps of boys who were separated from the larger group in order to help them develop more quickly as dancers. Talking about his early training, Corvino said that Pouyanne was a very good teacher who demonstrated steps and allowed him to pick them up at his own pace. Despite his athletic prowess, he remembered the exercises as being very strenuous. Pouyanne would demonstrate a step, make corrections, and manually move his students into correct positions when necessary. He stressed alignment (the adjustment of the body by line in order to allow it to work efficiently), placement (the positioning of different parts of the body to achieve correct posture), and plasticity (the pliable and flexible shaping and shifting of the bodily form). There was little talk. The class just watched Pouyanne and imitated each step.

Corvino's Stylistic Influences

According to Corvino, Pouyanne's style was a mix of elements taught at the school of the Paris Opera Ballet and Cecchetti technique, although Pouyanne did not identify these sources to his students. His musical knowledge and ability also infused his teaching. Corvino, Pouyanne's star pupil, absorbed his teacher's musicality into his own body, informing and enhancing his own approach to dancing and, eventually, to teaching. Influenced by Isadora Duncan, Pouyanne often included in his classes sections in which he improvised to music and had his pupils follow his lead. Out of this unfettered and free-associative process emerged some of Pouyanne's most distinctive and innovative choreography. It was with two solos created by Pouyanne that Corvino later auditioned for the Ballets Jooss, the innovative German company.

Classical ballet is a visual art built upon a technique that incorporates certain clearly defined elements of style. All classical ballet movement is performed with serenity and ease, while maintaining an element of precision and a clear sense of line. The five basic positions of the arms and legs in relation to the body were first codified by Pierre Beauchamps, who worked in the French court and at the Paris Opera. His balletic formulations became the basis for the technique taught at the ballet school of the Paris Opera, established in 1661 by Louis XIV.

There is a tendency among ballet dancers to refer to the French, Russian, Italian, and more recently, English, American, and Danish styles of ballet, especially when referring to the teaching or training of an individual. These different national approaches can be compared to different dialects of the same language. Today, the distinctions between them are often blurred in an international style. At the time Alfredo Corvino was training, however, the French were renowned in the dance world for their elegance and good manners, the Italians for their steely precision, and the Russians for their forceful, dramatic bravura.

Only later in his career, when he was formulating his own ideas about teaching, did Corvino recognize some of the distinctive variations in national style. It was not until he had to teach the approach of the Italian ballet master Enrico Cecchetti that he realized Cecchetti's approach had in fact been an important part of his training with Pouyanne.

Cecchetti (1850–1928), often cited as one of the greatest teachers in the history of ballet, taught in Italy, Russia, and England. His technique, noted for its attention to liveliness in the upper body and in footwork, in addition to an adherence to a strict routine of classroom exercises, built upon many of the concepts of the Danish teacher and choreographer August Bournonville (1805–1879). In turn,

Bournonville's approach, still visible in the unique style of the Royal Danish Ballet, was influenced by the French Romantic style of the 1830s. The Danish style is known for its understated yet warm elegance, its buoyancy, and its brilliant footwork. The Paris Opera Ballet School in the twentieth century was dominated first by the Italians and then by the Italian-influenced Russians. Hence, Corvino's early dance education included many interwoven approaches to classical ballet technique.

Pouyanne's studio was a very popular place, and visiting artists came to take classes, rehearse, and occasionally teach. There was a Cecchetti-trained English dancer named Vera Dalton, who came and taught Alfredo to partner her in the Petipa/Ivanov *Swan Lake* (Tchaikovsky) and in a *pas de deux* to Fritz Kreisler's music. She also taught him the shoulder lift from the "Bluebird Pas de Deux" from Petipa's *Sleeping Beauty* (Tchaikovsky). Corvino had already begun to learn how to partner from Pouyanne, but it was Dalton who taught him what was important from the female perspective, thus allowing him to further develop and refine his partnering skills. According to Corvino, Dalton resembled the English actress Vivian Leigh, and teacher and pupil had a brief affair outside of the studio. On occasion, other dancers, who had studied with a Russian dancer in Buenos Aires, would teach Corvino new combinations, often more athletic than the ones he had learned from Pouyanne, helping him to expand his basic dance vocabulary. He also took classes in classical Spanish dance.

Once Corvino became involved in dance, all his free time was spent in the studio, where he practiced endlessly on his own. He would repeat a movement or a step over and over until it felt right in his body—and it was, inevitably, correct. He would often select one of the many twelve-inch records in the studio's collection, play it on the turntable, and dance to the music.

One night, while practicing *changement*, Corvino inadvertently beat his feet together and thought he had invented a new step— *entrechat quatre*! Someone informed him that this was not in fact an innovative step, but he relished telling the story throughout his life, illustrating his belief that the body would develop and progress by itself—organically and inexorably—through the process of disciplined, dedicated, and correct practice. Corvino was strong, and had a natural *ballon*, a high jump, and an inbred musicality. Furthermore, through the constant repetition of the movements, he eventually became thoroughly familiar with them and in tune with his own body, thereby discovering the natural ease needed to perform even the most difficult of steps. This habit of working alone, which he continued throughout his years of performance, provided Corvino with a solid foundation of movement experience and physical (self) knowledge upon which to build both his dancing and teaching skills.

Corvino's Early Performing Career

Corvino started to perform after he had been studying dance for only about a year. Many of the embassies in Montevideo booked the "local" ballet group for entertainment at parties. The ensemble was composed of Pouyanne's students to whom he had taught sections of the nineteenth-century classical ballets as well as more contemporary works like *Les Sylphides* (Chopin), choreographed by Fokine in 1908. They performed indoors and outdoors.

In 1929, the progressive government of Uruguay created the Servicio Oficial de Difusión Radio Eléctrica (SODRE, translated as the Official Service of Radio Broadcasts). Conceived as a cultural broadcasting arm of the government, it established programs in theater, cinema, music (orchestral, choral, and opera), and eventually, ballet. In June 1931, SODRE took possession of the Teatro Urquiza, which it renamed Estudio Auditorio. The first concert there, a few weeks later, was given by the Montevideo Symphony Orchestra under the leadership of Vicente Pablo.

The Italian musician, composer, and conductor Lamberto Baldi became the first official director of the SODRE orchestra and chorus in 1932. Baldi had immigrated to South America as a young man in 1926 and subsequently taught and conducted in Brazil. He worked with SODRE until 1942 and again in the early 1950s before moving to Buenos Aires and Lisbon. He returned to Montevideo at the end of his life, and a plaza was named in his honor in 2004. It was Baldi who invited Pouyanne to create a professional ballet company, and he became the guiding light to the Corps de Ballet of SODRE, which was created on August 25, 1935, by government resolution number 4599. Admission to the company was to be by audition, and the maximum age of the dancers was set at twenty. Pouyanne moved his studio to the theater, where it eventually became the National School of Ballet, a magnet for local and visiting dancers.

In November 1935, the corps gave its first public presentation in the Estudio Auditorio. It offered the premier of *Nocturno Nativo* (*Native Night*). Choreographed by Pouyanne to music by Vicente Ascone and based on a libretto by Victor Pérez Petit, the director of the theater, it was the first Uruguayan ballet to be based on a national theme. It began with dancers and a guitar player sitting around a fire. The plot involved *gauchos*, or cowboys, and native fauna—birds and beasts from the *pampas*, the grassy plains of South America. Corvino danced the role of a puma and was required to leap from the wings to center stage. He said it was then that he discovered that he had a big elevation. Thus, at age nineteen, Corvino began his professional career as a dancer and performed featured roles from the very beginning.

Corvino remained with the company, earning a year-round salary, until the autumn of 1940. A contemporary flyer in the Corvino archives advertises a recital featuring students of the National Academy of Ballet, directed by Alfredo Corvino and Alberto Pouyanne, on Saturday, December 21, 1940, at 6:00 PM in the Estudio Auditorio. Pouyanne choreographed all the works, but Corvino had obviously already progressed from teaching children to directing a performance. In both of these endeavors, he was encouraged by Pouyanne, but Corvino never revealed any further details concerning these early teaching and directing activities or how they came to pass.

Performing in operas and in the many varied venues in Montevideo, the Ballet del SODRE developed a repertory that included *Sleeping Beauty* (Tchaikovsky), *Pulcinella* (Stravinsky), *Three-Cornered Hat* (De Falla), and other works that Pouyanne choreographed or reconstructed, based on his knowledge or memory of earlier productions. A program from 1937 testifies that for the Temporada de Ballets (Festival of Ballets) presented at the Estudio Auditorio, Pouyanne choreographed six works:

Pulcinella (Stravinsky), *Istar* (D'Indy), *La Noche en el Monte Calvo* (*Night on Bald Mountain*; Mussorgsky), *La Péri* (*The Flower of Immortality*; Dukas), *La Isla de los Ceibos* (*The Island of the Ceibos*; Fabini), and *El Festín de la Araña* (*The Party of the Spider*; Roussel). Corvino, listed as one of six primero dancers, performed in *Pulcinella*, *Istar*, *La Isla*, and *El Festín*.

In *Pulcinella*, Corvino danced the lead, leaping, laughing, and irrepressibly expressing his mad love for Pimpinella and, in turn, plumbing the depths of his hurt and sorrow when that love goes unrequited. Corvino remembered enjoying this role tremendously because of its potent combination of dance and emotion. In *Istar*, based on the symphonic poem of the same title about the beautiful and ferocious Babylonian goddess of fertility, love, and war, Corvino was one of the seven guardians of the gates of the Underworld. Istar was danced by Elsa Barabino, with whom Corvino remembered having an affair, commenting that she was very pretty.

La Isla de los Ceibos, a ballet that includes vague elements of pre-creation mythology, takes its name from the ceibo, the national flower of Uruguay. The ballet has four main characters: La Forma, the form or entity; La Savia, the intellect, which can transform time into a flower; El Ser, the being born in the forgotten zone; and El Paisaje, the landscape. The program notes read as a kind of metaphysical meditation, comparing the landscape of the mind to that of the entire earth and ruminating on the search for truth in the forgotten place of the soul, a destination to which we never truly arrive. La Forma exists within an infinite dreamscape that is without boundaries or clearly defined edges (e.g., the landscape), and El Ser represents the axle of love that joins form and knowledge. Corvino danced El Ser, which he called a "strong" role, and remembered that it was exciting to be onstage with Pouyanne, who danced La Forma.

El Festín is a ballet mime in which the spider tries to catch the other "party guests" in its web. The cast includes active, agile ants, beetles, a butterfly, worms, and, of course, a spider that performs a savage and cruel dance. Corvino played a praying mantis, which, with his female counterpart, attacks and destroys the spider.

Several of these ballets are described in *Detrás Del Telón* (*Behind the Curtain*), a book by Roberto Campos published in 1955, probably in Argentina. Campos was one of the young men who studied with Corvino under Pouyanne and danced as a member of the Corps de Ballet in the earliest performances of the SODRE company. He later went on to dance at the Teatro Colón in Buenos Aires. Campos gave a copy of his book to Corvino on November 11, 1999, with the inscription: "In spite of the long time that has passed, I have remembered, my friend and companion Alfredo, those difficult beginnings of the chosen art." In the book, he recalls Corvino's departure to the Ballets Jooss and says it gave him hope that one day he, too, would go on to bigger and better opportunities.

Some time after 1938, Pouyanne invited his former teacher Gala Chabelska to Montevideo. She had danced with the Diaghilev Ballets Russes and spent the years 1932–1938 dancing with René Blum and Colonel Vassili de Basil's company, the Ballets Russes de Monte Carlo. (Eventually, the two partners would split, and Blum would continue to run the Ballets Russes de Monte Carlo, while Col. de Basil would form a competing company called the Original Ballets Russes.) Chabelska first became known to the Montevideo dance community in 1920, when she and her sister performed in Montevideo and Buenos Aires, dancing in the ballets of Fokine, among others. After her arrival in Montevideo, Chabelska, in addition to her choreographing and teaching duties, also staged her own version of some of Fokine's works.

Montevideo's Other Dance Traditions

In addition to classical ballet, Montevideo had other traditions related to dance, and Corvino would assimilate and synthesize these influences and reflect them back in his own performances, teaching, and choreography. The most notable of these traditions was the celebration of Carnaval. This annual festivity was officially held on the Monday and Tuesday preceding Ash Wednesday, but observances usually took place throughout the entire week, with many shops and businesses closed for the duration. Launched formally by representatives of the government, Carnaval involved much humor and color and included open-air performances and *tabladas*, or living tableaux.

An important part of Carnaval was the *Desfile de Llamadas* (Parade of Calls), whose origins stretched back more than 200 years to the arrival of African slaves in Uruguay. Similar to the more well-known Carnaval celebrations of Rio de Janiero, the Parade of Calls is composed of *comparsa*, neighborhood groups of dancers and musicians performing *candombe*, a uniquely Uruguayan musical form for three drums that evolved from African drumming rhythms. Most prevalent during Carnaval, it could also occasionally be heard and seen on Sunday nights in the streets and nightclubs of Montevideo. The standard, archetypal characters in these performances were the Old Mother, the Broom Man, a Young Woman, and a Witch Doctor, all interacting in the satiric style typical of many African songs and stories. Yet this venerable folkloric tradition could occasionally make room for modern innovations. In the 1940s, a character based on the popular American singer and dancer Josephine Baker entered the repertory.

Though strongly associated with Argentina, the tango developed in a parallel manner in Uruguay as well. In both countries, the dance was based on the *milonga*, a South American style of song that incorporated improvisation (a contest called *payada*, in which two singers with guitars take turns improvising, is still an important part of Uruguayan cultural life). When dance steps were set to it, the tango, a sensual, partner dance form, resulted. Carlos Gardel, a famous tango musician, was from Uruguay, as were many others. The Uruguayan poet Horacio Ferrer wrote the lyrics for several tangos by the famous Argentinean composer Astor Piazzolla.

Montevideo and Buenos Aires as Cultural Communities

Aside from the city's dance scene, Montevideo provided Corvino with a rich store of cultural vitality, intellectual energy, literary sophistication, and artistic refinement. Its proximity to South America's preeminent cultural capital, Buenos Aires, also ensured that some of the world's greatest dance troupes and choreographers passed through Montevideo with some regularity, furthering Corvino's professional and artistic education and exposing him to the dance world's newest ideas and most refined artistry.

The city that nurtured and showcased Corvino and his fellow young dancers was both beautiful and sophisticated. Montevideo, the largest city in Uruguay, is the southernmost national capital on the South American continent. Situated on a hill and surrounded by water on three sides, it enjoys a warm but not hot climate year-round. It has a busy port, wonderful beaches, and the most interesting and varied architecture in South America. Almost all the streets in the old city have a view of the water, some from both ends. The broad, tree-lined boulevards, the beautiful parks, and the botanical garden appear today much as they did in Corvino's time.

Most of Montevideo's architectural treasures date from the nine-teenth and early twentieth centuries, and Corvino lived and worked among them. The National History Museum, built in 1900, is the former residence of the country's first president. Similarly, the Palacio Taranco, a sprawling 1910 mansion, is now home to the Museum of Decorative Arts. In Plaza Independencia, the main square at the edge of the old city, a twenty-six-story skyscraper (completed in 1928 and often compared to a multistage rocket) boldly thrusts upward. The National Bank, built in 1924, with its five-foot-wide marble columns and six-inch-thick brass doors, has been compared to New York's Grand Central Station. The National Library of Uruguay (1816), the Museum of Natural History (1837), and the National Museum of Fine Arts (1911) are also fine examples of the city's elegant architecture.

There is a strong enough French influence on this architecture to have led a travel reporter for the *New York Daily News* to write in April 1966: "In the old city . . . there are whole blocks that look as if they had been lifted from Paris." An article in the *New York Times* on October 15, 2006, describing the city that is now viewed as a gateway to the nearby and very trendy Punta del Este beach resort, says: "Like Uruguayans, [Montevideo] sits back and reveals itself little by little."

During Corvino's early years as a dancer, in the 1920s and 1930s, roughly half of Uruguay's population resided in Montevideo. With an extremely high literacy rate and a large middle class, the city was known for its sophisticated contributions to literature, music, and art.

Montevideo was increasingly known not only as a cosmopolitan cultural center but also as a modern metropolis. Though horse-drawn carts and carriages were still present, Montevideo also boasted electric trolley cars and a growing number of automobiles. Buenos Aires, just across the river in Argentina and a bit larger, was close enough to allow people—as well as cultural ideas and influences—to flow freely between the two cities.

Both cities had large French and Italian populations, the enriching influence of indigenous music and dance, and the tradition of the *gaucho* in art and folklore, as well as their citizens' deep appreciation of art, theater, music, and dance. Uruguay also enjoys a rich tradition in the literary arts. José Enrique Rodó is one of the nation's most significant literary figures. His essay *Ariel* (1900) stresses the importance of the spiritual over the materialistic and urges resistance to the cultural and political dominance of Europe and the United States. Among playwrights, Florencio Sánchez's early twentieth-century works deal with Uruguay's social problems. Horacio Quiroga is renowned for his short stories and Juan Zorrilla de San Martín, Juana de Ibarbourou, and Delmira Augustini for their poetry.

The Teatro Solís (1856) in Montevideo, one of the most prized and celebrated opera houses in South America, and the Teatro Colón in Buenos Aires (originally constructed in 1847 and rebuilt in 1888) both hosted leading international performance companies as well as individual artists. Corvino was part of the enthusiastic audience for the city's musical offerings. He saw Marian Anderson, the African American contralto who was forbidden to sing in Constitution Hall in Washington, D.C., because of her race and performed instead on the steps of the Lincoln Memorial for an audience of more than 75,000. Jascha Heifetz, the Russian-born violinist, perhaps the greatest of the mid-twentieth century, also entertained audiences, including Corvino, in Montevideo.

The Diaghilev Ballets Russes (1909–1929) came to Rio de Janeiro, Montevideo, and Buenos Aires on its first South American tour in 1913 and returned to the region at least twice afterward. This avant-garde company, under the direction of Sergei Diaghilev, was responsible for changing the face of twentieth-century ballet and made a deep and lasting impression on South American audiences. Its repertory, a collaborative mixture of the work of contemporary artists, composers, librettists, dancers, and choreographers—among them Igor Stravinsky, Pablo Picasso, and Michel Fokine—was composed of colorful, rhythmical, and emotionally driven ballets, often based on Russian characters or themes. On the company's first trip to South America, it brought along Vaslav Nijinsky, the charismatic Polish/Russian dancer known for his technical virtuosity and his ability to *become* whatever character he was dancing, and Tamara Karsavina, the beautiful, delicate, and versatile ballerina.

Anna Pavlova, the Russian ballerina whose name was synonymous with ballet and who toured the world in order to make her art more widely seen and known, was among those dance artists who brought ballet companies to Buenos Aires in 1917. She spent most of World War I in South America.

The ballet company at the Teatro Colón was established in 1925. Amply stocked with well-trained dancers, it commissioned works by many leading European choreographers. Bronislava Nijinska, the first female ballet choreographer of the twentieth century, was a member of Diaghilev's company and the sister of Nijinsky. She was an innovative choreographer who ventured beyond the classical ballet genre. She created six ballets for the Colón company in 1926 and two in 1927. She also choreographed for the operas presented there.

Michel Fokine came to the Colón company in 1931. He restaged his works *Scheherazade* (Rimsky-Korsakov), *Les Sylphides* (Chopin), *Polovtsian Dances* from *Prince Igor* (Borodin), *Firebird* (Stravinsky), *Le Spectre de la Rose* (Weber), and *Carnaval* (Schumann), all part of the original Ballets Russes repertory. He also created new versions of his ballets *The Adventures of Harlequin* (Beethoven) and *The Sorcerer's Apprentice* (Dukas).

Corvino remembered seeing performances by La Argentina, the dancer born in Buenos Aires who is credited with the development of Spanish dance as an art form. He was also exposed to the work of Harald Kreutzberg, the German dancer, choreographer, and teacher known for the theatricality and humor of his work. Kreutzberg founded the Ballet Madrid in 1932 with Federico García Lorca and Alexandre and Clotilde Sakharov, who lived for a time in Montevideo. The Russian Alexandre and German Clotilde toured widely together in a program of elaborately costumed solos. Alexandre Sakharov described these works, choreographed in a static, angular movement style, as "abstract mime," though they were often emotionally charged as well.

There were large French and Russian colonies in Montevideo, and these expatriates brought their children, especially the girls, to take ballet classes at the National School. There was always a Saturday afternoon tea at the theater, attended by dancers and painters and accompanied by live music. Corvino recalled that practically all the adults in the room had seen Pavlova, Nijinsky, and the Ballets Russes, and they talked endlessly about them. As a result of being immersed in all this passionate conversation, Nijinsky became Corvino's idol. Pouyanne, Corvino, and his fellow dance students would try to see every dance company and production that appeared in Buenos Aires. And what could not be seen in person could be imaginatively brought to life by library books. The opportunities to receive an education in the arts in Montevideo were many, and as a result, the city's populace included an increasingly sophisticated dance audience.

Alberto Pouyanne remained influential in Montevideo for a little more than a decade, but by 1947, others had taken over, including Chabelska and Alexandre Sakharov. The latter, with whom Pouyanne was friendly, brought with him fresh ideas that began to influence what eventually became a distinct group of young modern dancers operating outside ballet. Over the years, Tamara Grigorieva, a Russian dancer who had performed with Col. de Basil's Original Ballets Russes, worked sporadically as ballet mistress to the SODRE company, as did María Ruanova, an Argentine ballerina who had studied with Nijinska and danced with René Blum's Ballets Russes de Monte Carlo. Yurek Shabelevsky, a Polish dancer who performed with de Basil and with Ballet Theatre, played a role in the SODRE company as well. In 1968, William Dollar, an American dancer and choreographer who trained with Fokine, came to teach and choreograph, bringing with him the influence of George Balanchine, the brilliant Russian-trained American choreographer, with whom he had studied and danced.

Thus ballet in Uruguay grew and developed steadily, but during Alfredo Corvino's training and early performance career, opportunities within the country remained limited. Many aspiring dancers thought about leaving, but few were able to do so.

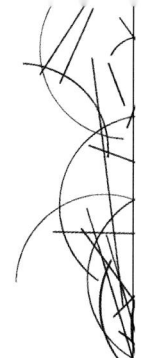
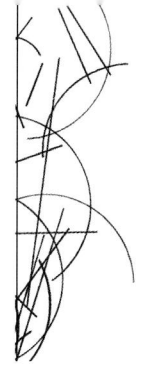

Chapter 2

ENTERING A LARGER WORLD OF DANCE THROUGH THE BALLETS JOOSS

The Ballets Jooss performed in Montevideo in late 1940. Corvino said that the members of the SODRE company were expected to see every group that danced in the city, and in Buenos Aires if possible. Since he had advance notice, Corvino read everything he could find about the company beforehand, and he was therefore already well acquainted with the work of Rudolf von Laban, Mary Wigman, Sigurd Leeder, and Kurt Jooss before he first saw them perform. He went to a performance of the company (or it might have been a rehearsal, Corvino could not remember) when he had a bad cold and a fever.

Jooss and Laban

Kurt Jooss (1901–1979) was simultaneously a product of German modern dance (known in central Europe as *Ausdruckstanz*) and a codifier of many of its concepts, particularly the ideas of Rudolf von Laban. German modern or expressionist dance rejected the technique of classical ballet and was instead based on a subjective outpouring of personal emotions. As such, it was closely related to the painting and literature of the time. It had no specific technique of its own but instead technique and style emanated from the individual performer or choreographer.

Rudolf von Laban (1879–1958), a dance theoretician, founded a school in Munich, Germany, in 1910. His most famous students were Mary Wigman, and Kurt Jooss. Laban believed that movement was valid and made sense only if it proceeded organically or sequentially from its source. To Laban, human movement was living architecture that had to obey the laws of balance. He saw the basic elements of orientation in space as up/down, forward/backward, and side/side, forming the three dimensions length, depth, and breadth. He understood the center of gravity of the standing body to be the spot at which the midpoints of the three dimensions meet.

Combining the qualities of two dimensions creates a plane. The up-downness of the vertical dimension combined with the side-sideness of the horizontal dimension creates the vertical plane. The forward-backness of the sagittal dimension combined with the up-downness of the vertical dimension creates the sagittal plane. And the side-sideness of the horizontal dimension combined with the forward-backness of the sagittal dimension creates the horizontal plane. Each plane has two diameters that bisect it along a pathway from one corner of the plane to its diagonal opposite. Laban proposed that all three planes and their diameters create spatial scaffoldings for movement.

Laban also referred to a "pure" diagonal as a spatial pathway crossing through the center of the body that stresses the qualities of all three dimensions equally. The cube as a three-dimensional form is the best way to visualize this. When standing inside this imaginary cube, the fully stretched body can reach from the corner of the cube that is above, behind, and to the right, and then move through the center to the corner that is below, forward, and to the left, thereby crossing all three planes and using all the basic directions simultaneously and equally. Laban felt that this was the most dynamically powerful line of movement through space.

Additionally, he developed theories related to the inner attitude of the dancer and the subsequent outer manifestation of this attitude. He felt that the dynamic aspects of movement were a direct result of the inner attitude or intention of the mover. Laban called these dynamic qualities of movement "Effort." He felt that all movements could be described in terms of four Effort factors: Flow, Weight, Space, and Time. Various combinations and degrees of these Effort factors were capable of creating a complete range of movement dynamics.

Fleeing Germany, Choreographing War

Kurt Jooss came from a musical family, and his early training in music preceded his studies with Laban, in whose company he danced. Jooss first studied ballet in Paris and Vienna. He believed in classical ballet as well as the new modern approach. He left Laban's company in 1924 and became ballet master at the Munster Opera. In 1927, he became director of the dance department of the Folkwang School in Essen, where, the following year, he founded an experimental theater group. This became the Ballets Jooss in 1932. The same year, he won an international choreographic competition in Paris with his work *The Green Table* (Cohen).

The roiling political storm clouds of Nazi Germany, however, soon erupted, putting an early end to Jooss's work in that country. Refusing demands to fire Jewish artists in his company, Jooss was forced to leave Germany in September 1933, fleeing just hours before the local Gestapo arrived to arrest him. By 1934, he and Sigurd Leeder, who had taught with him at the Folkwang School, were codirecting the company and school at Dartington Hall in South Devon, England. Five teachers from Essen joined him, as did Laban several years later. Dartington became a cultural institution that greatly influenced dance education in England and, through Jooss and Leeder, the emerging English ballet.

The Green Table, with piano music by Frederick Cohen, is Jooss's most famous work. An antiwar ballet, it begins with a group of men wearing tuxedos and large masks bearing exaggerated expressions, talking around a rectangular table covered in green baize. These caricatures of diplomats converse and argue in highly stylized movements to the strains of a playful tango. Their negotiations come to an abrupt end with the ear-splitting sound of gunshots from revolvers pulled from their jacket pockets and discharged into the air, signaling that peace efforts have failed and war has been declared. In the following scenes of battle, one sees soldiers on both sides of the conflict; women of all ages and temperaments; the War Profiteer, who takes advantage of everyone; and Death, the most memorable character of all. Portrayed as a vital part of life, Death embraces all genders, classes, and occupations.

He is extremely democratic in his manner of taking human life. After all these scenes of death and destruction, the dance ends with the men in tuxedos at the green table again (or still) arguing selfishly and senselessly.

Joining the Ballets Jooss

During his first encounter with the Ballets Jooss, Corvino sat in the balcony and saw Rudolf Pescht, a senior dancer in the company, dance the role of Death in *The Green Table*. The impact of this ballet remained with him throughout his life, and he sometimes wondered if his senses were heightened and made more receptive that night due to his fever.

The Ballets Jooss toured North America for fourteen weeks in 1940. While waiting for Jooss and Leeder to join them from England, where they were detained due to their German passports, the group embarked on a six-week tour of South America under the guidance of the Russian impresario Leonid Greanin. This trip was planned to be brief, yet it turned into an amazing and prolonged journey that lasted thirteen months and included just about every country in South America, with the exception of Paraguay and Bolivia, and every travel, living, and eating experience possible. By the time the company arrived in Uruguay, several dancers had left and returned to Great Britain to take part in World War II. Thus, to fill these suddenly available slots, the Ballets Jooss held an audition in Montevideo.

Pouyanne encouraged Corvino to try out for the renowned company, which was offering six-month contracts. He felt that the experience would be invaluable for his pupil, who would undoubtedly return a better and more experienced dancer. Corvino auditioned with two solos choreographed by Pouyanne, which he danced on the stage of the Auditorio. Because Corvino knew everyone who worked at the theater, he was able to put on a fully lit and costumed performance to recorded music. As a result, he was accepted into the company. In the autumn of 1940, Corvino left Montevideo to enter what he described as "a new world." He was twenty-four years old and, except for short visits to Buenos Aires, had never left Uruguay.

Corvino's first contract with the Jooss company, dated September 24, 1940, was for six weeks commencing October 1. It stipulated that he was to receive ten shillings per day, the same as all the other members of the company. The director assumed the responsibility of paying Corvino's travel expenses back to Montevideo. It was presumably after this initial contract expired that, having been deemed acceptable, Corvino received his first six-month contract, and then a second and probably a third.

The Jooss company operated as a cooperative, with everyone receiving an equal salary and sharing the same travel and living conditions. Cut off from it roots in Germany, and now exiled from its newly adopted home base in England while touring throughout South America, the members of this close-knit, egalitarian, commune-like environment embraced Corvino, taught him, and nurtured him. In retrospect, Corvino called it the best time in his professional life, and he was completely happy with the Jooss dancers. The ensemble came from all over—England, Latvia, Russia, Hungary, Switzerland, Holland, Germany, and Austria. Corvino was the only one who did not speak English, but among the Babel of languages, there were some dancers who spoke Spanish. He said his English always retained a slight German accent because he began learning it from these dancers.

Corvino's Continuing Education

The company Corvino joined was still biding its time until Jooss and Leeder could join them. In the interim, Frederick Cohen, who was actually the musical director as well as the cofounder of the company, took over as artistic director. The indefatigable Greanin somehow got them from place to place. Though the tour was being greeted by enthusiastic audiences, the company was badly in need of new repertory. Since the war prevented them from touring in Europe, it was felt that an infusion of new ballets would allow them to tour North America again, with a new program. Jooss never made it across the ocean, in part because he and Leeder were interned in London as enemy aliens. Then, upon their release, they were unable to attain visas. Thus, it was not until the 1950s, when Corvino went to teach in Essen, Germany, that he and Jooss actually met.

Corvino took company classes every day with Hans Zullig and Lydia Kocers. Zullig was a Swiss dancer, teacher, and choreographer who had studied in Essen with Jooss and Leeder and was a soloist with the company from 1935 to 1947. He later went to Chile. As a teacher, he tried to identify each individual student's distinctive way of moving and thinking and work with that, within the demands of a technique related to the anatomy of the body. Kocers, also known by her married name, Lydia Franklin, was born in Russia. She grew up in Riga, Latvia, where she studied ballet and a form of modern dance based on the work of Isadora Duncan. Her modern dance teacher sent her to Dartington Hall. She eventually moved to the United States, dancing with Agnes de Mille. Kocers and her husband later opened a ballet school in Caracas, Venezuela, that was free to all, bringing dance to all sectors of society.

Under the tutelage of Elsa Kahl, a dancer and Frederick Cohen's wife, Corvino also took a daily class in Dalcroze Eurhythmics. Before Laban's theories began to spread throughout Europe, the only real choice for those who wished to train as dancers but did not wish to become classical ballet dancers was Dalcroze Eurhythmics. Émile Jaques-Dalcroze was a Swiss music teacher who, upon discovering that many musicians had no real understanding of rhythm, developed a system of training them by translating musical rhythms into body movements. In 1911, he established a school in Hellerau, near Dresden, Germany, which eventually had its own company. Mary Wigman, later a pupil of Laban's and a leading figure in German modern dance, studied with Dalcroze. Other prominent individuals in the central European dance movement of the 1920s and 1930s also studied with both Dalcroze and Laban.

Kahl, who called Corvino "Little Pescado," after a big, black fish called a Corvina, gave him private lessons. She believed that, histori-cally, Dalcroze was the link between ballet and Laban's concepts of space and Effort dynamics. Corvino was learning these techniques, concepts, and philosophies bit by bit, as he learned roles and rehearsed with the Jooss company. He had no problems with the expressive qualities of the movement because of his training with Pouyanne. He followed his already established way of learning—look carefully, listen, and reproduce the combination.

Jooss and Leeder had worked to consolidate a system of teaching based on Laban's ideas and principles. To this, they added ballet, from which they took not only the technique but also some of the teaching methods. Jooss's classes were a cross between the freedom and subjectivity found in Expressionist dance and the objectivity and adherence to certain principles and forms that he found in ballet. Much of the intellectual thinking of the time also reflected these two viewpoints. Classes began at the *barre* and used *pliés*, but they also incorporated Laban's idea of the diagonal in its two-dimensional and three-dimensional forms.

Corvino always remembered this use of the diagonal and the Jooss method of developing combinations by adding one step to another. He was also greatly influenced by the many three-dimensional circular movements based on the Laban diagonal, in which the three spatial pulls experienced throughout the body create a highly mobile form that pulls the body off balance and into motion. To Jooss, artistic intention alone was the factor that determined the vocabulary used in a given ballet, and he sought to train dancers who would be capable of understanding and performing any movement required of and essential to the specific ballet and its unique expression. Hence, his and Leeder's classes combined the spatial and dynamic explorations of Laban's work with the verticality and precision of ballet.

Corvino enjoyed the musicality, the changes of dynamics that ballet dancers sometimes forgot about, and the total expressivity of the entire body. He admired many of the more experienced dancers in the Ballets Jooss and was intrigued by Hans Zullig, who had what Corvino remembered as a magnificent mastery over his body.

Various seasoned members of the company, including Lucas Hoving, took over the job of directing rehearsals. Hoving was born in Holland, where he studied with Yvonne Georgi, a German modern dancer, and later with Jooss at Dartington Hall. He eventually settled in the United

States, where he danced with Martha Graham and Valerie Bettis and had a long association with the José Limón Dance Company. He also choreographed and taught at the Juilliard School, among other places.

Corvino found the ballets performed by the Jooss company emotionally satisfying and thrilling to dance. He felt that there was never an extraneous movement in a Jooss piece. Choreographically, Jooss believed in austerity, eliminating anything superfluous or merely decorative. The dramatic narrative came first, determining the form and movements of the dance. Sometimes a work resembled classical ballet. At other times, a work partook more of Laban's style. Still other dances featured Jooss's unique synthesis of both influences. He wanted the structure and clarity of ballet, but his close observations of the minute subtleties of a particular character were often portrayed in terms of Laban's spatial configurations, as well as his notions of the dynamic Efforts (e.g., what would be the attitude of this particular character toward Weight and Space?).

The South American Tour

After performing in Montevideo, the Ballets Jooss continued its tour of South America, and Alfredo Corvino began the experience of a life-time. The first place the company performed after leaving Montevideo was Buenos Aires. Then they crossed the Andes en route to Chile, where Corvino, wonder-struck, saw snow for the first time in his life. While in Chile, he was napping before one of the performances and woke up to find his bed on the other side of the room. Thinking nothing of it, he went to the theater and danced as usual, even though there was almost no one in the audience. It was only later that the dancers discovered that there had been an earthquake earlier that day. Corvino had apparently slept right through it!

By means of boats, buses, and trains, the company traveled along the coast of South America. Corvino vividly recalled one day in Bolivia, when the company set out in a bus for a day trip. When they arrived at their supposed destination, the dancers confusedly realized that it was the same venue they had departed from that morning! The roads had been built by prisoners and were lined with crosses, presumably marking the graves of the workers who had died during their construction. The driver of the bus, evidently confused and disoriented by the overwhelming number of crosses clotting the roadside, unknowingly followed the road back to its starting point.

When the Ballets Jooss got to Caracas, Venezuela, Corvino's contract was almost up, and he was asked to remain with the company for another six months so that he could join them on the planned North American tour. Corvino's talented presence was especially valuable and needed because so many British nationals were leaving to return home and join the armed forces. The company was also losing one of its most central and long-standing members. Ernst Uthoff had studied with Laban, Jooss, and Leeder and left Germany with the Ballets Jooss. While touring South America with the company, however, he and his wife, Lola Botka, decided to remain in Chile, where they opened a school at the university in Santiago that would eventually become the Chilean National Ballet. Uthoff and Botka's company included many Jooss works in its repertory. Joined later by other former Ballets Jooss members, they spread Jooss's teaching methods and dance philosophy throughout South America.

Meanwhile, what remained of the Ballets Jooss had to wait because, with the exception of Corvino, who came from a neutral country, the dancers did not have the visas necessary to perform in the United States. Any other dance company might have begun to show the strain of the uncertainty of existing in this protracted limbo, but the Ballets Jooss remained a true ensemble, always welcoming new members into the group. They rented a large empty villa in the middle of Caracas where they rehearsed in the hall and the dining room. Corvino would often head out onto the porch alone to practice, but a number of the other dancers usually joined him. Expatriate English and Americans invited the dancers to their swimming pools and occasionally fed them. Among the Jooss ballets presented during this time (and later in the United States) in which Corvino had a role were *The Big City*, *Ball in Old Vienna*, *The Seven Heroes*, *The Green Table*, *A Spring Tale*, *The Prodigal Son*, and *Ballade*.

The Big City, with music by Alexander Tansman, was a twenty-four-minute depiction of urban loneliness and disillusion. Using a realistic approach, with the curtain left open during scene changes, it was a human tragedy showing the disparity between the rich and the poor. In *Ball in Old Vienna*, Joseph Lanner's music accompanied a humorous, carefree, plotless work that showcased waltzing couples (one of which included Corvino) at an 1840s ball. *The Seven Heroes*, originally set to Henry Purcell's music and revised by Frederick Cohen in 1937, was a comic ballet based on a fairy tale by the Brothers Grimm. It included a pair of young lovers, an irate mother, seven brave men who "embark on adventure," and a wedding. Corvino danced the role of the husband of the Woman with the Fork.

A Spring Tale, set to Cohen's music, was a romantic ballet in four acts, involving a prince and his friends, who set out in quest of a bride. The ballet also featured a queen and her court, several nights spent in a forest (one with a hermit), and a happy ending. Corvino danced the part of a wood witch. *Ballade* was based on a French song describing love intrigues at a Baroque-era court. John Colman, a pupil of Dalcroze's, composed the music. The choreography was more ornamental than was usual for Jooss. Corvino danced the role of a gentleman of the court.

The Ballets Jooss Joins New York's Dance Scene

After more than a year spent touring South America and waiting for entry visas, the Ballets Jooss finally arrived in New York City on June 11, 1941, aboard the Grace Line's ship the *Santa Paula*. They were installed in a rooming house on Sixth Avenue and 12th Street and also rented a loft, where they cleaned and repaired the wooden floor so they could rehearse. Their initial performance on September 22—the company's first in the city since 1938—opened a five-week season at the Maxine Elliott Theatre. This was followed by a week at the Locust Street

Theatre in Philadelphia, and then a return to New York for two weeks at the Windsor Theater at 157 West 48th Street.

Corvino arrived in a country with a population of almost 138 million, which, the previous November, had elected Franklin Delano Roosevelt to an unprecedented third term as president. Just prior to his reelection, FDR had declared that American soldiers would not go to war, and most United States citizens considered themselves too far removed from Europe's problems to be overly concerned with this latest "European conflict." Since then, however, Adolf Hitler's armies had overrun and now controlled most of western Europe. The United States, although technically neutral, was quietly lending noncombat assistance and support to the Allied forces and was being drawn ever onward toward all-out involvement.

The country was far less embroiled in wartime hysteria than it had been during World War I, despite the fact that the first peacetime program of compulsory military service in U.S. history—a draft—was instituted with the passage of the Selective Service Act in 1940. All men between the ages of twenty-one and thirty-six had to register for this draft. The Priorities Act of the same year authorized the federal government to force manufacturers to accept defense orders over civilian ones. The Office of Civilian Defense, which would train millions of Americans as air raid wardens, guards, firefighters, and members of coastal air patrols, had also been created.

The Alien Registration Act of 1940 required the registration and fingerprinting of all aliens residing in the United States, of which Corvino was one of approximately five million. Although technically not at war in June 1941, the United States was building its army; increasing its manufacture of arms, battleships, and warplanes; sending goods and ships to Great Britain to help bolster its defense against German air attacks; lending war materials to friendly nations; and generally preparing itself for the declaration of war on Japan, Germany, and Italy that finally came in the wake of the Japanese attack on Pearl Harbor, Hawaii, on December 7, 1941.

Most of these activities, except for the Alien Registration Act, did not affect Corvino. Many Latin American nations declared war on the

Axis powers, but Uruguay had remained neutral. Corvino was more concerned with dancing with the Jooss company, trying to attune his ear to a new language, and exploring New York City. In New York, business was again booming as the Depression's stranglehold was finally broken, and pinup photos of the Hollywood stars Rita Hayworth and Betty Grable were ubiquitous. Women were wearing colored woolen stockings or *trompe l'oeil* leg makeup because silk was being rationed. Floppy hats were all the rage.

On Broadway, where a popular form of music, dance, and dramatic performance that Corvino was also interested in reigned, one could see the Rodgers and Hart musical *Pal Joey* (the score of which included the song "Bewitched, Bothered, and Bewildered"), the first production of the comic murder mystery *Arsenic and Old Lace*, and Noel Coward's delightful and effervescent *Blithe Spirit*.

In dance, the Ballet Russe de Monte Carlo, now based in New York, was the most popular touring company in the United States and had been giving regular seasons in New York since the late 1930s. Ballet Theatre (later to become American Ballet Theatre), under Lucia Chase and Richard Pleasant, was dedicated both to preserving classic ballets and encouraging new choreography. The company was not quite a year and a half old and had already signed up the dance luminaries Michel Fokine and Antony Tudor. George Balanchine, recruited by Lincoln Kirstein to develop an American ballet culture, had been in the United States since 1933, and the School of American Ballet, founded by the two men, had been in New York since 1934. There were several companies intermittently associated with the school, but it was Kirstein and Balanchine's last joint venture, Ballet Society (formed in 1946), that eventually became the New York City Ballet. Italians usually ruled the Metropolitan Opera Ballet and School, although the American Ballet, under Balanchine and Kirstein, was the resident company there from 1935 until 1938. There were numerous ballet studios in the city, most of them run by Russians.

Many of the American modern dance pioneers of the 1930s, among them Martha Graham, Doris Humphrey, Charles Weidman, and Helen Tamiris, were teaching and giving occasional performances in the city, as was the German-trained Hanya Holm. In the 1940s, New York City was becoming an important and vital international center of dance.

When in New York, the Jooss repertory included many works seen before in the city, chief among them *The Green Table*, which was danced at every performance at the Windsor Theater. The most noted Jooss works new to New York were *Chronica*, with music by Berthold Goldschmidt, and *The Prodigal Son*, originally set to the music of Prokofiev but revised in 1937 with Cohen's music.

Chronica is about a medieval-era dictator of a European town, but there was little doubt that the character represented Hitler. *The Prodigal Son*, in which, deviating from the biblical source, the son is brought down by his pursuit of power, not hedonistic living, was praised for its simple, stylized poignancy. The reviews in both New York and Philadelphia were glowing and enthusiastic, with special attention paid to the smooth ensemble dancing of the company. The welcome was warm, and the houses full.

Drums Sound in Hackensack (1941), a brand-new ballet and the first piece in the Jooss repertory by someone not associated with the company, was choreographed by Agnes de Mille, assisted by the iconoclastic modern dancer Sybil Shearer. De Mille, the American dancer, chore-ographer, and sharp-tongued writer (and niece of the Hollywood director Cecil B. DeMille), was raised in California. She went to London, where she studied with Marie Rambert and Antony Tudor and created dances for concerts and a revue. She was associated with Ballet Theatre from its beginnings and would create the American-themed ballet *Rodeo* (Copland) for the Ballet Russe the year after working with the Jooss company. This work brought her enormous attention and served as her entrée into musical theater.

Corvino's strongest recollection when asked about his experience working with de Mille centered upon one particular day when the company was rehearsing onstage in New York. A young woman came to see them, and she was introduced as Miss de Mille. The Jooss dancers were then told that they were going to start a new ballet with her. Rehearsals began the very next day, and Corvino found the work extremely difficult.

Billed as a taste of Americana, *Drums Sound in Hackensack* takes place on a farm outside of New Amsterdam (the Dutch colony that would become New York City). The Dutch settlers get the Indians drunk and steal their furs. In return, the Indians return in war regalia to retaliate. In a ballet within the ballet, called "The Unhappy Premonition," the Dutch farmer's young daughter reveals her understanding of the wickedness taking place. As a mixture of conscience and comedy, the critics found the work interesting if not always successful. They generally liked Frederick Cohen's music, based on old Dutch songs. John Martin, the dance critic of the *New York Times* and a strong advocate of dance as an art form (particularly modern dance), felt de Mille had superimposed an alien style on the dancers. Others noted that the prominent solos altered the unified demeanor of the company, previously its signature strength.

Corvino agreed with Martin. In the role of an Indian, he had to draw near a girl who was carrying a jug on her shoulder. He was supposed to take the jug while twisting his legs around each other. But he could never do it and kept falling backward, dropping the jug. Although he thought his legs were too short for this maneuver, he finally came to master the step. Recounting the story with much laughter, Corvino added that he asked de Mille if the movement was supposed to be comical. She never gave him an answer.

During the third week of January 1942, the Ballets Jooss, engaged by the Shubert Organization, began a series of performances in which it presented a half hour of repertory on a bill shared with the Boston Comic Opera Company, which was presenting Gilbert and Sullivan operettas. The Shubert Organization was a theater syndicate formed in the late nineteenth century by the three Shubert brothers—Sam, Lee, and Jacob—who started operating in New York City in 1900. By the late 1920s, they owned more than 100 theaters nationally, including the Shubert, the Broadhurst, the Booth, and the Barrymore in New York City. They usually presented light entertainment such as musicals and operettas.

Arthur Sullivan, the English composer, along with his compatriot, the librettist W. S. Gilbert, created a distinctive form of British comic operetta that parodied late nineteenth-century politics and social mores. Gilbert's satirical wit and ingenious use of simple words were matched by Sullivan's infectious melodies and use of widely popular opera music to enhance the parody. They were very popular in the United States, and their work was presented by many performing groups.

In a series of programs that ran until mid-March, a Jooss ballet was paired with a Gilbert and Sullivan work: *The Green Table* with *HMS Pinafore*; *The Big City* and *Ball in Old Vienna* with *The Mikado*; *The Prodigal Son* with *The Pirates of Penzance*; *Drums Sound in Hackensack* with *Iolanthe*; *Seven Heroes* with *The Gondoliers*. Even though he was consumed with preparing for his own dancing with the Ballets Jooss, Corvino found the time to take in these Gilbert and Sullivan performances and marvel at their dense plotting (often hinging on mistaken identities or disguise), vivid characterization, political and social satire, romantic comedy, intricate word play, and sparkling, effervescent music. Corvino absorbed it all.

In spring 1942, Lucas Hoving choreographed a piece for the Holland Classic Circus, which was then appearing in New Jersey. A wealthy Dutchman who was a friend of Hoving's owned this traditional European one-ring horse circus. He had brought the circus to the United States from the Netherlands to protect it from the invading Germans and the escalating war in Europe. Hoving invited Corvino, a few other Jooss dancers, and Ann Hutchinson to perform his dance on a small stage and then walk around the horses.

Hutchinson, an American who grew up in England, had studied with Jooss and Leeder at Dartington Hall. There she notated several Jooss ballets using Laban's system of writing dance, known as Kinetographie Laban in Europe and Labanotation in America. She then moved to New York, where she performed in concerts and on Broadway and was active in establishing the Dance Notation Bureau. She later returned to England, married the dance historian Ivor Guest, and has since published and taught extensively in the area of dance notation. She remembers that following the New Jersey performance, the combined circus and dance troupe toured New England.

The End of the Road

Although a fourth transcontinental tour had been planned and newspapers had reported that the Ballets Jooss was set to tour the Shubert theaters nationwide, All Arts Productions stopped sponsoring the company. As a result, the Ballets Jooss, as it existed in New York, disbanded in June 1942. Some members returned to England (where there were plans to reorganize the company), some went to Chile, and some remained in the United States. Greanin, who had been with the Ballets Jooss since the early thirties, ended his connection with the company. Frederick Cohen and Elsa Kahl remained in New York City, where Cohen eventually headed the Opera Division at the Juilliard School and Kahl taught Dalcroze Eurhythmics.

The Jooss dancers who returned to England did so via a special arrangement with the British government, which gave them single passages in convoys crossing the Atlantic. The reformulated company would return to New York in December 1946, with Jooss, but Corvino was in Germany at the time and did not see them.

Corvino said he would have remained with the Ballets Jooss as long as it was performing. When Greanin gave him $150 for passage back to Montevideo, as stipulated in his contract, Corvino realized that this would be just enough to buy a cheap ticket on what he termed a "banana boat." He told Greanin he would rather stay in the United States. The Russian told him he was crazy to think he could make his way in New York, with little money and even less command of the English language, but Corvino had made his decision.

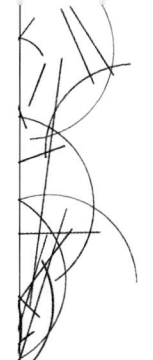

Chapter 3

Joining Both
the Ballet Russe
and the U.S. Army

Corvino's decision to remain in the United States was based in part on a meeting he had had in 1938 or 1939 with Léonide Massine, the Russian choreographer, ballet master, and dancer. A graduate of the Bolshoi School, Massine joined the Diaghilev Ballets Russes in 1914, when he was brought in to replace Vaslav Nijinsky. He subsequently began his choreographic career as Diaghilev's protégé. Massine continued to work with the various incarnations of the company after Diaghilev's death in 1929.

At one time the most famous choreographer in the world, Massine's best-known ballets include *Le Tricorne* (de Falla), *Parade* (Satie), and *Gaîté Parisienne* (Offenbach, arr. Rosenthal), as well as others based on classical symphonies. Countless generations of cinephiles know him best for his choreography and performance as Ljubov, the choreographer in the beloved 1948 dance film *The Red Shoes*.

At the time of Corvino and Massine's encounter, the Ballet Russe de Monte Carlo was performing in Buenos Aires. According to Corvino, this was the company every dancer in the world wished to join. One day during its run, he snuck into the balcony of the theater to watch the troupe. He was not disappointed by the rehearsal of Frederick Ashton's *Devil's Holiday* (Tommasini), with Frederic Franklin in the lead, or by the subsequent performance he attended with his teacher, Pouyanne.

Fighting Over a Renowned Company

At this time, the Ballet Russe de Monte Carlo, one of the myriad descendants of the Diaghlev Ballets Russes, was under the managing directorship of Sergei Denham, with Massine as artistic director. Originally based in Monte Carlo, it moved permanently to New York in 1939, following the outbreak of World War II.

After Diaghilev's death, the dancers and repertory scattered, in spite of the best efforts of René Blum, who was in charge of the Monte Carlo Opera House, which legally owned the Ballets Russes name and the repertoire. It took Blum two years to form a new company, with the help of Colonel Vassili de Basil. The Blum/de Basil company lasted until 1935, performing the Diaghilev repertory. Then Blum, disgusted with his autocratic partner, left.

De Basil eventually formed his own company, as did Blum. At one point, they were both performing in London at the same time, offering the same ballets. There were lawsuits and countersuits over the rights to the name Monte Carlo, as dancers and choreographers, including Fokine and Massine, switched from one company to the other.

Finally, Blum sold the rights to the Monte Carlo name and repertory to Denham, an ally of Massine's, who wanted to head his own company. Denham, a Russian-born impresario and banker, was vice president of World Art, the company that, technically, bought the name and repertory rights. World Art, later known as Universal Art, was formed by a group of wealthy patrons (including Jules Fleishman) who were backing Massine in his attempt to leave de Basil. Denham remained as director of the Ballet Russe de Monte Carlo for twenty-four years. Col. de Basil's company became known as the Original Ballets Russes.

Preparing for the Ballet Russe Audition

Prior to the Ballet Russe de Monte Carlo's performances in Buenos Aires, the boat on which the dancers were traveling docked in Montevideo, where they rehearsed for a brief time. How Pouyanne knew Massine is unknown, but he took Corvino to the boat to arrange an introduction. Corvino clearly remembered Massine drinking *maté*, a type of tea that is still consumed through a silver straw in that part of the world. Massine told Corvino that if the young dancer ever came to New York, he would audition him. Massine felt he could not do so in South America, partly because he did not have the money to pay for Covino's voyage to the United States. The young dancer did not have the funds either.

Three years later, however, Corvino had finally arrived in the United States. Having decided to stay in New York and remembering Massine's pledge, Corvino next set about finding a way to sustain himself during the summer of 1942 and preparing for an audition with the great choreographer in the fall. In order to save money, he left the room he had been renting while he was a member of the Ballets Jooss and moved to one in the home of Arlene Momeyer on West 36th Street. Now deprived of the help he had received from members of the Jooss company, who had served as intermediaries when language became a problem, Corvino was forced to blunder forward on his own. He used his limited English, resorted to French if he was really in trouble, and ate at the Horn and Hardart Automat on West 57th Street, where he did not have to speak to order his meal.

The automat was a gleaming chrome and glass emporium, where one could change a dollar bill for nickels, quarters, and dimes. Food of every sort was displayed on shelves behind little glass doors. By inserting the proper amount of money (indicated next to the chrome knob), the lock automatically opened, and one could retrieve such items as a sandwich, baked beans, chocolate pudding, milk, or macaroni and cheese. The food could then be carried to a nearby table. None of this operation required the utterance of a single word, and the clientele was representative of every possible type and class of New York citizen, high and low.

To prepare for his audition, Corvino first went to the School of American Ballet, where he took nine classes, some of them with Muriel Stuart. Aesthetically, however, he felt completely lost there. Stuart was a British dancer who had studied with Cecchetti and Pavlova and danced with the latter's company. She was coauthor with Lincoln Kirstein of *The Classic Ballet: Basic Technique and Terminology* (Knopf, 1952).

Corvino's most positive memory of this brief period at the School of American Ballet was meeting Fred Danieli, one of his first friends in the United States, who, at different times, studied with Fokine, Anatole Vilzak, and Antony Tudor. Danieli later became the director of the Garden State Ballet in New Jersey.

Feeling uninspired and lacking the money to continue at the School of American Ballet, Corvino turned to Greanin. Fortunately, Greanin knew Anatole Chujoy, the director of the Vilzak/Schollar School in Steinway Hall on 57th Street, just down the street from Carnegie Hall. Chujoy succeeded in getting Corvino a scholarship to study there.

Anatole Vilzak and his wife, Ludmila Schollar, were both graduates of the Imperial Ballet School in St. Petersburg. They had danced with the Maryinsky company (now known outside of Russia as the Kirov Ballet), and with Diaghilev's Ballets Russes when Michel Fokine and Vaslav Nijinsky were choreographers and Enrico Cecchetti was the ballet master. Vilzak had also danced in many of Bronislava Nijinska's works while in the Ida Rubinstein Company. Rubinstein was a Russian dancer, actress, and director, and a private student of Fokine's who had joined the Diaghilev company in 1909. Due to her beauty and acting ability, she danced the title roles in Fokine's ballets *Cléopâtre* (Arensky) and *Scheherazade* (Rimsky-Korsakov). She first formed her own company in 1911 and commissioned lavish works from leading choreographers, designers, and composers.

Both Vilzak and Schollar had spent time in Buenos Aires working with Nijinska at the Teatro Colón. With Fokine and Nijinsky as his main influences, Vilzak's classes were precise, musical, and dramatically motivated, and required a dancer to think. He was also known as a brilliant partner. A number of dancers from the Ballet Russe de Monte Carlo, including André Eglevsky, studied with him.

Sometime during that summer of 1942, a friend brought Corvino to the studio of Vincenzo Celli, whom Corvino later called "the son of Cecchetti." Celli was an Italian who had immigrated to Chicago, where he studied with Adolph Bolm. He had then returned to Italy to study with Cecchetti, becoming the last of that master's favorite pupils. Celli went on to become the ballet master of the Ballet Russe de Monte Carlo from 1938 to 1940 and was considered the American authority on Cecchetti. A strict and feared teacher, Celli counted among his students the ballerinas Alicia Markova and Mia Slavenska. Lacking money, Corvino took only one class from this master of Cecchetti technique in New York. It was a void in his training he would always regret.

Most of Corvino's energies were spent upon the three classes a day he took with Vilzak. At the end of each day, he would go home and record the entire lesson, in English, in a small 3" x 7" leather-bound notebook with lined pages. He filled a total of seven notebooks with these class notes, and he kept them always. He did not remember ever consulting them later, but the very act of writing down each step and exercise must have fixed them securely in his mind.

Eugene Loring came to observe some of Vilzak's classes and invited Corvino and a few others to perform with his group, Dance Players. Loring studied theater and then ballet with Balanchine, Vilzak, and Stuart. He was a dancer with the Fokine Ballet in New York, Balanchine's American Ballet, and Kirstein's Ballet Caravan, and a soloist with Ballet Theatre. He choreographed for the latter two, as well as for Hollywood films. Many of his ballets had American themes and characters.

Loring eventually founded his own school in California, where he was concerned with training the complete dancer, one able to perform all styles and genres. He was the founder, lead dancer, and choreographer of Dance Players, which was in existence from 1941 to 1942. The troupe had a three-week engagement in Pennsylvania, where they stayed on a farm owned by Winthrop Bushnell Palmer. She was the cofounder of the company and wrote the scenario for and danced in one of the pieces performed. She also wrote the book *Theatrical Dancing in America: The Development of Ballet from 1900* (Bernard Ackerman, 1945) and was an editor of the publication *Dance News*, as well as a poet and playwright.

Along with Loring's work, the program for the Pennsylvania performances also included *Jinx*, choreographed by Lew Christensen to music by Benjamin Britten. Christensen later staged this ballet for the New York City Ballet in 1944 and the San Francisco Ballet in 1949. Christensen, the youngest and best technician of the three dancing

Christensen brothers from Utah, danced for Balanchine at the Met and for all of the pre–New York City Ballet Balanchine/Kirstein companies, for which he also choreographed. He was the first American to dance Balanchine's *Apollo*. Christensen spent most of his later career in San Francisco with his brothers, teaching and choreographing more than seventy ballets for the San Francisco Ballet School and company.

In addition to Corvino, the cast for the Dance Players performances in Pennsylvania included Janet Reed, Joan McCracken, Zachary Solov, and Michael Kidd. Reed studied with Christensen, Balanchine, and Tudor. She would go on to dance with Ballet Theatre, where she originated the role of the *First Woman*, in Jerome Robbins's breakthrough ballet, *Fancy Free* (Bernstein), on Broadway and with the New York City Ballet, where she was also a ballet mistress. At one point, Reed was the artistic director of the Pacific Northwest Ballet.

Joan McCracken had studied with Loring, danced with Ballet Caravan, and was one of the original members of Ballet Theatre. She starred in many Broadway musicals, including *Oklahoma!* and several Hollywood movies.

Zachary Solov trained in Philadelphia, became a soloist with Ballet Theatre, and later choreographed for the Metropolitan Opera Ballet from 1951 to 1958, during which time Corvino danced there.

Michael Kidd, who danced with the American Ballet and Ballet Caravan, also went on to Ballet Theatre. He later became a very successful choreographer on Broadway, where he choreographed *Finian's Rainbow*, *Guys and Dolls*, and *Can-Can*, among others. Kidd also choreographed several Hollywood musicals, including *Seven Brides for Seven Brothers*.

The Audition

The United States had entered World War II in December 1941, following the Japanese bombing of Pearl Harbor in Hawaii. By the summer of 1942, American planes were bombing the Pacific Islands and Axis-controlled territory in Europe, the U.S. Marines had invaded and seized the Japanese-occupied island of Guadalcanal, and U.S. forces had also invaded North Africa. Rationing of certain foods—sugar, coffee, meat, butter—and other goods needed for the war effort, including gasoline, rubber, and metal, had been put into effect. Government agencies had taken over most aspects of life, including housing, shipping, transportation, and scientific research. Women were moving out of the house and into manufacturing jobs related to the war industry, and African Americans were migrating from the South into the more industrial cities of the North in large numbers.

Whether Corvino was really aware of all these international developments and domestic flux is unknown. He might have been cognizant of the fact that Irving Berlin's popular show *This Is the Army* was playing on Broadway and the Pulitzer Prize for drama had gone to Thornton Wilder's play *The Skin of Our Teeth*. The most popular musical comedy of the year was *By Jupiter*, starring Ray Bolger, while George Gershwin's landmark operetta *Porgy and Bess* had its first performances.

When Corvino returned to New York following his work with Loring's Dance Players in Pennsylvania, he continued studying on scholarship with Vilzak until he auditioned with Massine for the Ballet Russe de Monte Carlo in September 1942. Corvino couldn't remember whom he contacted or how the audition came about, but he did remember that Frederic Franklin conducted it. He also remembered that Massine, who watched the audition, really liked him because he exhibited the ability to dance everything—from the classics, to Fokine, to Massine's own choreography. How he knew this Corvino did not say, although he implied that Massine spoke to him directly (an explanation corroborated sixty years later by Franklin). Eglevsky, who also observed the audition, cast the deciding vote that granted Corvino admission into the company. Corvino also did not reveal how he knew about the vote of Eglevsky, an acquaintance from Vilzak's studio.

While he was waiting to hear from the Ballet Russe, Corvino also auditioned for the Metropolitan Opera Ballet. He was invited to join the company but turned them down, taking a chance on his hoped-for acceptance from Massine. His gamble paid off, and in October 1942, Corvino joined the Ballet Russe de Monte Carlo.

Chico Enters the Ballet Russe Fold

Corvino's first contract, the American Guild of Musical Artists' (AGMA) standard dancers agreement, dated October 29, 1942, was for nine weeks only, from November 2, 1942, to January 2, 1943. One of these weeks would be a rehearsal week (earning Corvino $22.50). The remaining eight performance weeks paid $45 per week. There was an option to engage Corvino again beginning on January 3, 1943, for thirteen additional weeks—four of rehearsal and nine of performance. His weight was listed as 127 pounds, and he pledged to keep himself in good physical condition.

Corvino did indeed please Massine enough to earn his contract extension. The second contract was signed on January 3, 1943. During the 1942 season, he changed his name to Korvinoff in order to appear Russian but soon changed it back to Corvino. At that time, because the public still viewed the Russians as being supreme in ballet, it was very common for dancers to "Russify" their names.

Frederic Franklin was ballet master of the Ballet Russe at the time of Corvino's admittance. He remembered that Corvino was a bit naïve and that his English was not great. He says they all understood each other, however, and the language barrier quickly became irrelevant, especially since some company members had been in Cuba and spoke Spanish. According to Franklin, Corvino was very gregarious and a fully integrated member of the company. One day, someone asked the newest company member what they should call him, since "Alfredo" seemed too formal for this group, so many of whose members had nicknames. Somehow the nickname "Chico" was settled upon. "Chico" means "young boy" in Spanish, and Corvino was known by this name forever after to those who had been in the company at the time. Franklin also recollected that Corvino was a very versatile and lively performer who could do anything he was given, and that in *Gaîté Parisienne* "he wore the gloves marvelously."

Corvino said he initially went into the ballets without proper rehearsal—the one week stipulated in his contract was hardly suffi-cient—and that his first partner in the company, Tatiana Chamié, an older dancer in the corps who eventually established her own studio in New York, broke him in. She had danced with the Diaghilev company, specializing in Massine's works. They were in *Gaîté* together.

During the two and a half years he was in the Ballet Russe, Corvino rose from the corps to solo roles, while traversing the United States half a dozen times. He roomed with Sviatoslav Toumine, whose nickname was Slava. When they checked into hotels, Corvino would wait with the bags while the very fleet Slava rushed ahead to get them the best possible room. His post-performance "crowd" consisted of Alan Banks, Nikita Talin, Peter Deign, and Herbert Bliss, and his memories were of much laughter. Banks later choreographed and formed his own company, the Brooklyn Civic Ballet. Talin went into teaching, and Bliss, who died in a car crash at thirty-seven, danced with the New York City Ballet. After one performance, Franklin recalled going out with Corvino and Armand Picon. The three of them drank gallons of ginger ale and drove the waiters crazy.

Corvino once joked that when he joined the Ballet Russe, they immediately gave him the roles no one else wanted. In all probability, it was his natural *ballon* and light quickness, and the company's urgent need for male dancers that allowed him immediately to gain the roles of a waiter and a soldier in *Gaîté Parisienne*, Massine's 1938 lighthearted romp about a glove seller and other habitués of a Paris café, danced to Offenbach's music. Corvino also danced the role of a child and the Trepak in *The Nutcracker* (Tchaikovsky), a cowhand in Agnes de Mille's breakthrough ballet *Rodeo* (Copland), and a peasant in Bronislava Nijinska's *Snow Maiden*. The latter, set to Alexander Glazounov's music, had a scenario by Sergei Denham (the company manager) and was based on a Russian fairy tale in which a snow maiden melts because she falls in love.

Later, Corvino's parts included the lead of the farm lad in Fokine's *Igrouchki* (Rimsky-Korsakov), the dance master in *Gaîté Parisienne*, and, with Leon Danielian, a pair of British sailors in *The Red Poppy* (Glière). *The Red Poppy* was Igor Schwezoff's adaptation of a revolutionary Russian ballet in which a capitalist oppresses a dancing girl. Schwezoff changed the capitalist to a Japanese bar owner and gave the girl British,

Russian, and American sailor friends. It was still propaganda, though of a pro-Western sort, and perhaps for this reason the audiences loved it. Corvino also danced Dr. Drosselmeyer and one of the Chinese dancers in *The Nutcracker.* Two other ballets choreographed by Fokine in which Corvino danced as a member of the corps were *Scheherazade*—the exotic and sensual story of the shah's favorite wife and her obsession with one of the male slaves—and *Polovtsian Dances* from Prince Igor (Borodin), in which the dancers display the spirited virility of medieval Russian warriors.

Corvino also appeared as a dandy in Massine's *Le Beau Danube* (Strauss)—a light, frivolous work that evokes a romantic Vienna—and as a village youth in Pilar López's *Cuckold's Fair* (Pittaluga). This ballet had a scenario by the Spanish writer Federico García Lorca dramatizing an old Spanish custom of sending a barren wife into the forest to search for verbena, which, if found, meant she would have a baby. The company had long performed *Coppélia,* or *The Girl with the Enamel Eyes,* choreographed in 1879 by Arthur Saint-Léon to Léo Delibes's music. In it, the heroine, Swanilda, is engaged to Franz, who is attracted to the mechanical doll Coppélia, a creation of Dr. Coppelius's. Swanilda pretends to be Coppélia, an imposture that seems to bring the doll to life, delighting Dr. Coppelius. He decides to try to take Franz's spirit and put it in his beloved doll, thereby threatening Franz's life. By the end of the ballet, all is set right again. Swanilda and Franz marry, and the whole village celebrates. Corvino danced the role of one of Franz's friends.

Opportunities Seized and Missed

Massine departed soon after Corvino's arrival at the Ballet Russe. Throughout Corvino's time with the company, it was basically without an artistic director. Additionally, others in the financial and management end of the company were leaving. As a result, Sol Hurok, who was booking both the Ballet Russe and Ballet Theatre, decided to drop the Ballet Russe. At times, the company would be touring in a city like

Chicago, and Denham would have arranged an engagement in an additional city, such as Cleveland, but he did not have the funds to send them there until the very last moment. One year, Ballet Theatre and the Ballet Russe were performing in New York at the same time, resulting in a sort of ballet war, not unlike the earlier one between Blum and de Basil. This sense of uncertainty, disruption, and barely controlled chaos had an effect on Corvino's development as a dancer and artist. In retrospect, Corvino felt that he would have benefited more artistically if there had been more consistent company leadership and less turmoil.

Both Nijinska and Balanchine spent substantial amounts of rehearsal and class time with the Ballet Russe, but neither was the resident choreographer until 1944, when Balanchine was given that post. He began the season by choreographing *Danses Concertantes*, set to Stravinsky's music. It premiered in September 1944, and Corvino danced the "Second Variation" with Ruthanna Boris and Dorothy Etheridge. Balanchine choreographed and restaged other works for the company during his two-year tenure, including *Mozartiana* (Tchaikovsky), *Concerto Barocco* (Bach), *Night Shadow* (Rieti), and *Le Bourgeois Gentilhomme* (Strauss). Corvino was also one of the Blackamoors in *Le Bourgeois Gentilhomme*. He remembered Balanchine being very pleasant to work with and wearing penny loafers with holes in the soles. In company class, he taught *frappés* as real strikes, the way Corvino always taught them afterward (unlike in Balanchine's own School of American Ballet, where, according to Corvino, that approach was discontinued).

Corvino remembered that during his time with the Ballet Russe, Balanchine always espoused the basic tenets of classicism—clarity, harmony, nobility—and the corps was an integral and necessary part of his ballets. By the time he left the Ballet Russe in 1946, Balanchine was ready to begin his reinvention of classical technique, which, with the New York City Ballet, changed American dance forever. Balanchine was certainly an important part of Corvino's ongoing dance education, but in 1945, a year before Balanchine's departure, Corvino was forced to leave the company due to the military draft. He always felt that he missed out on much that he might have learned from Balanchine.

Nijinska was working steadily and inspired many at the Ballet Russe, but the apex of her creativity had already been reached prior to

45

the time that Corvino was with the company. Corvino danced in her abstract ballet *Chopin Concerto*, which used eighteen women and six men in what John Martin of the *New York Times* characterized as one of the three best ballets of 1942–43. Corvino was also a Tartar warrior and a buffoon in her ballet *Ancient Russia* (Tchaikovsky), an unsuccessful work about Russian women rescued from Tartar captors. Denham had asked her to create this piece because he hated to waste the sets that were designed by the artist Nathalie Goncharova for a failed Russian-themed ballet of Massine's. Corvino remembered the battle scene in *Ancient Russia* that was danced with real sabers. Once during rehearsal, when Corvino got cut on the chin and stopped to look at his wound in the mirror, he remembered Nijinska asking, "Does he think he's pretty?"

Corvino said that Nijinska was partial to the Russians in the company and thought every mistake they made was someone else's fault. He recalled that in class, when a dancer passed her in a *grand jeté*, she would place her hand on the dancer's back and shove him or her into the air. She also demonstrated certain concepts of centering and going into the air by lifting a pole. Since he remembered this clearly, it is possible that this method of illustration inspired his use of the same prop later in his own teaching.

In June 1944, while the company was on layoff, Balanchine staged five dances for *Song of Norway*, a musical based on the life of the Norwegian composer Edvard Grieg. The show opened in Los Angeles (sponsored by the Los Angeles Civic Light Opera), traveled to San Francisco, and eventually went on to the Imperial Theatre in New York, where it was scheduled to play for two weeks in August. The dancing ensemble of eleven men and eleven women, including Corvino, all drawn from the Ballet Russe de Monte Carlo, was led by Alexandra Danilova and Frederic Franklin. Danilova, Russian born and trained, was prima ballerina of the Ballet Russe from 1938 until 1945. Vivacious and elegant on stage and off, "Choura," as she was called, was a guest with many companies, danced with the Diaghilev company, staged works, and taught at the School of American Ballet from 1964 to 1989.

Franklin studied in his native England and in Paris. He started dancing in cabaret and was a soloist with the Markova-Dolin company before joining the Ballet Russe in 1938 as a principal dancer. His direction and staging of ballets all over the world has been enhanced by his phenomenal memory, versatility as a performer, consideration as a partner, and dedication to his art. Danilova and Franklin were a sparkling pair onstage, displaying a rare and convincing chemistry. Their dancing could range from romantic to comic, but it was always done fully, precisely, and at the highest energy level, enchanting audiences throughout the world. Corvino always remembered them in performance with delight.

Song of Norway was so successful that the run in New York was extended. Ultimately, the dancers had to be replaced so that they could rehearse for the upcoming regular Ballet Russe season. The same year, *On the Town*, written by Betty Comden and Adolph Green and choreographed by the newcomer Jerome Robbins, joined *Song of Norway* on Broadway.

Maria Tallchief, also a member of the *Song of Norway* cast, was one of four American stars of the Ballet Russe at this time. A Native American from the Osage tribe and born in Oklahoma, Tallchief studied in Los Angeles with Nijinska and, later, at the School of American Ballet. She was a brilliant technician whom audiences adored. She was a leading ballerina with the New York City Ballet, where she became Balanchine's muse and his third wife.

Tallchief and Corvino often took class together with David Lichine. Lichine was a Russian-born dancer who had studied in Paris with Nijinska, among others. He danced with the companies of Anna Pavlova and Ida Rubinstein before becoming a principal in 1932 with the Ballets Russes de Monte Carlo. He stayed with the company under its various names until 1941 and later joined Ballet Theatre. As a choreographer, his most famous work was *Graduation Ball* (Strauss, arr. Dorati). Of Jewish ancestry, Lichine was reportedly terrified when performing in Nazi-era Germany with de Basil's company. Corvino recalled that sometimes in class Lichine would set up a competition between himself and other male dancers to see how many turns or jumps they could execute or how high off the floor they could soar. Lichine would often let this go on for up to an hour and then call it a draw. Corvino found this challenging and fun.

It is possible that had Corvino spent more time with the Ballet Russe, he would have been given more and larger roles, but the United States Army intervened.

Entering the Army

In the spring of 1945, while much of the world was still embroiled in the waning days of World War II, the Ballet Russe was enjoying a weekend off after performing in New Haven, Connecticut. Corvino went to the company's office in New York to pick up his mail and found a draft notice instructing him to report for induction at his local draft board on May 8, 1945. His scheduled induction day happened to be the day after the generals of the Third Reich surrendered, thereby ending the war in Europe. Nevertheless, Corvino dutifully reported to Fort Dix, New Jersey.

The draft notice was not a complete surprise. In 1944, Corvino's draft status had changed from neutral alien to allied alien due to the fact that Uruguay had abandoned its stance of neutrality in favor of the Allied cause. This political shift made Corvino, as a single male of twenty-nine, eligible for the draft. His first induction date had been put off, thanks to some string-pulling by Sergei Denham. Corvino had saved his copy of a letter written by Denham to Local Draft Board No. 20, at 331 Madison Avenue, dated March 6, 1945. As a special favor, Denham, who desperately needed every one of the few male dancers he still had, requested that the draft board allow Corvino to travel to Canada as part of a Ballet Russe tour, if the company guaranteed that the dancer would return to the United States by April 22, 1945. Permission was granted.

There was no more putting off the draft, however, and Corvino was forced to leave the Ballet Russe and report for military service. In a letter from Corvino to Denham dated June 5, 1945, he asked Denham for his last paycheck, since his hasty departure for Fort Dix prevented him from picking it up at the Ballet Russe office. A letter in the

Corvino archives from the U.S. Immigration and Naturalization Service (INS) dated June 4, 1945, states that Corvino had been granted an extension of his admission to the United States until May 10, 1946. The INS was apparently unaware that Corvino had been drafted and was serving in the U.S. Army. A June 16, 1945, letter from a secretary in the Ballet Russe office (at 130 West 56th Street) to Corvino states that the office had received a copy of the letter described above from the INS, asks him to write and let them know how he is getting along, and gives Corvino Freddie's (Frederic Franklin) address in Florida, where Corvino was receiving his basic training.

On the basis of a telegram Corvino sent to Dr. Juan Carlos Blanco, the Uruguayan ambassador to the United States, dated May 15, 1945, with a return address c/o the Uruguayan consul in New York, it can be concluded that Corvino appealed to Uruguay to get him out of the United States Army. Corvino asked the ambassador to intervene in order to get the draft board to revoke the order for his induction the next day. He made his argument based on the fact that he held a Uruguayan passport and a contract with SODRE in Montevideo. Corvino, possibly with the help of the consul in New York, had contacted SODRE earlier, and they had sent him a contract of employment dated April 30, 1945. A copy of this hastily drafted contract had been sent to Washington, D.C., along with Corvino's Uruguayan passport.

The answer to this telegram came in a letter dated May 18, 1945, from Ramón Piriz-Coelho, writing on behalf of the ambassador. Piriz-Coelho wrote that, according to U.S. law, Corvino must serve, but that it was possible that in the next few months there might be an agreement between Uruguay and the United States that would enable him to serve in the Uruguayan army instead. Additionally, Corvino's contract with SODRE did not exempt him from this military service. He returned Corvino's passport and the contract, both sent to Corvino c/o the consulate in New York.

Rivas Costa, the Uruguayan consul in New York, sent Corvino a letter at Camp Blanding, Florida, dated May 31, 1945, informing him of the answer from Washington and telling him he would wait for official word as to how to proceed. On June 3, Corvino wrote to Piriz-Coelho, thanking him and vowing to serve in the military of Uruguay if given an opportunity to do so. He also wrote to Rivas Costa in New York, acknowledging the receipt of the correspondence from Washington and indicating that he understood that his present situation depended on a change of relationship between the two countries. Corvino kept handwritten copies of the two letters he had sent, written on paper printed "United States Army."

On August 23, there was a note from Juan Yriart, a secretary in the Embassy of Uruguay, telling Corvino that they have received a letter from Montevideo inquiring about his possible discharge from the U.S. Army and asking for more information. However, in the Corvino archives in which these letters were found, there is no more official correspondence, possibly an indication that Corvino gave up this plan of action and decided to accept his American army assignment. On August 6, the United States dropped the first atomic bomb on Hiroshima, Japan, followed by a second one on Nagasaki three days later. On August 15, Emperor Hirohito surrendered to the Allied Powers, and on September 2, the Japanese formally signed the Instrument of Surrender. Hence Pvt. Corvino was now serving in the army of a country no longer at war.

The Mannheim Soldier Show Workshop

Corvino remembered enjoying the calisthenics during his basic training at Camp Blanding in Jacksonville, Florida. He wanted to be a paratrooper but was too short. During basic training, Corvino some-how received a cut on his shin, which became infected, causing him to be hospitalized. Consequently, his unit was shipped out to the Pacific without him. He was given an unexpected two-week furlough and then sent to Germany via France.

Classified as an entertainment specialist in Special Services, Corvino initially went to Heidelberg, where he spent most of his time guarding equipment, gasoline, and ammunition in the cold and damp weather. Then he was sent to Mannheim, where, as a member of Special Services, he was occupied with dancing in shows produced by the Mannheim Soldier Show Workshop. For example, in *The Doughgirls*, starring the actress Arlene Francis, Corvino played a bellhop. He also served as a director and choreographer, creating entertainment for the troops and taking these shows on the road, traveling in a large truck throughout western Europe. In either Heidelberg or Mannheim, there was an opera house across the street from the Red Cross canteen. He asked a porter at the theater if they had a ballet company. The answer was in the affirmative, and Corvino was soon invited to take a class there. Shortly thereafter, he was asked to teach it.

One of his off-duty excursions while in Europe was to go skiing in Switzerland with a group of friends. He went up a mountain and saw a sign he interpreted as "beginners." An absolute novice, he went flying down the slope, turning around as he got to the bottom and coming to a snow-spraying halt in a backward position. As it turned out, this was actually a racecourse, and a race was under way. The sign had not said "Beginners" but "Beginning." Corvino received a medal for his daring and accomplished maiden ski run!

Alberto Pouyanne wrote to Corvino in September and October of 1945, indicating that he had received letters from him. In one letter, Pouyanne says that he had seen Corvino's mother and sister, and that the money Corvino had left in Pouyanne's care for them had run out. Corvino also kept a letter from his fellow dancer and friend Omar in Montevideo, expressing Omar's hope that Alfredo was safe and would eventually return to his country. His cousin Humberto wrote at the same time to his "dear cousin Pocho" and talked about some of their childhood memories. This correspondence indicates that others knew of his attempt to get out of the army and return to Uruguay and to SODRE, and they offered their universal encouragement of such a course of action.

Corvino's life in the service, however, was going along pleasantly enough and seemingly without strain. He had even obtained a hunting and fishing license for "Land Greater Hesse," good from April 1, 1946, to March 31, 1947.

A Criminal Scheme and a Mystery Woman

During this time period, Corvino was confined to the military stockade awaiting the outcome of a court-martial. The facts are a bit murky, but evidently one of the men in the unit was on night duty when he found the forms used to change army script into dollars. Someone was needed to forge a signature, and Corvino wrote someone else's name on the paper when requested to do so. One of the girls in the workshop show found out and reported the incident. As a result, Corvino and two other soldiers, including the mastermind of the scheme, were placed under house arrest while the investigation took place, then court-martialed, and sent to the stockade for 140 days to await the verdict.

The first time anyone in New York heard about this incident seems to have been in October 1946, when a letter was sent to a woman named Ruth Rose from a soldier identifying himself as someone who had known Alfredo for eight months and referring to circumstances that had them both confined to an army stockade. The mysterious letter writer states that Corvino would never do anything wrong and that Corvino had spoken to him about Ruth and told him of their correspondence. The letter writer, believing that he and Ruth shared a loving concern for Corvino, then speaks ominously about the toll these developments had taken on their mutual friend:

> This episode has not only changed his outlook on life, but also Alfredo . . . The ideals and things that once meant so much to him have blown up in his face. He won't begin to be himself again until after this mess is over and he has returned to civilian life. Alfredo has done what he always does when he is in trouble. He has withdrawn himself into a protective shell . . . [N]othing . . . anybody could do will help.[1]

There is no name attached to this perceptive plea for help. In response, Ruth Rose wrote on October 15, 1946, to the "Commanding Officer," asking that Pfc. Alfredo Corvino be given a fair and equal chance to prove his innocence. On October 16, she wrote to Alexandra

---

1 From the Corvino archives.

Danilova regarding "Chico," whom she referred to as her fiancé, asking if company members would sign a petition she had written and enclosed.

Shortly afterward, there is a note to Sergei Denham's secretary, Peggy, from another secretary named Janet, who also worked in the Ballet Russe office and had known Corvino previously. Janet enclosed a copy of a letter from Franklin to Danilova, saying that, instead of having the company members sign Rose's petition, he felt it would be best if Denham wrote a letter to Corvino's commanding officer attesting to Corvino's good behavior while in the Ballet Russe. Janet also suggested to Peggy that Danilova contact Rose, since no one at the Ballet Russe knew who she was.

Denham wrote a letter, dated October 30, 1946, to the judge advocate of the 20th Special Service Company, saying that the Ballet Russe had always found Corvino to be of good character and, not knowing the nature of the offense, wished to be enlightened on the subject. A reply on November 6, 1946, reporting that the trial had already taken place but the verdict was not yet known was signed by Benny Williams, 1st Lt. Commanding. Denham sent a copy of this letter to Ruth Rose.

The final verdict exonerated Corvino. He received an honorable discharge on March 6, 1947, and he returned to New York via Fort Dix. Years later, when asked about this curious incident, Corvino's wife, Marcella, blamed her husband's naïveté and said that the incident really centered upon other soldiers in the unit who were buying things in the PX and trying to smuggle them back to the States. Corvino himself remained genuinely puzzled by the whole bizarre sequence of events and, on the whole, remained silent about it.

The mystery of Ruth Rose, however, has been mostly cleared up. Corvino kept several letters he received during that autumn of 1946, all of them found after his death. One was sent to "Pete and Al." Another began, "Hello, there, Al," and sends regards to Peter and Fred. Written and sent by former Special Service buddies, the letters indicate knowledge of the stockade situation and cheerily seem to expect the imminent release of the three court-martialed soldiers—Peter, Fred, and Alfredo. There is also a letter from Ruth Hazan, a civilian actress technician who was in *Doughgirls*, dated October 23, 1946. In it she says that "they"—presumably those in charge of the stockade—would not let her visit Corvino and that "we have been court-martialed as well." Hazan's letter says that many members of the cast spoke to Corvino's defense counsel, who was confident that "all three of you" would be free within a month. She says she is going home, offers to send him money if he needs it, wonders if he gets to practice at all, and asks, "Would you like me to call Marcella or Ruth?" The letter ends, "And you Alfredo Corvino Dolce, call me in N.Y.—and for now—please write. Love, Ruthie."

Thus, several people knew that he was writing to both Marcella Rubin (his future wife, whom he had met at a photo shoot at City Center in 1943) and the mystery woman Ruth Rose. When pressed, Corvino said that it was customary during this time for people to house soldiers on leave, and that on one of his furloughs he had spent ten days in the home of a Miss Rose, a divorcée to whom he had been introduced. They had an affair and kept in touch via letters. She had quickly fallen in love with Corvino and thought it was reciprocated. Yet during the unexpected leave he was given before he was sent overseas, he spent most, if not all, of his time with Marcella, and it was evidently then that their friendship had become love.

Corvino saved one letter from Ruth Rose, who was probably a balletomane, dated November 13, 1946. The letter shows that she spoke Spanish. She notes that she received a letter from his mother and sister Margarita, and asks why he does not write to his mother or to her. She says that she has had many recent problems in addition to Corvino and his absence, that it seems as though she is writing to the dead when she writes to him, that his last letter was "so icy," and now he doesn't write at all. She expresses her love and impatience.

How or why Corvino's mother had Ruth Rose's address is unknown, as is whether or not he had any contact with her when he returned to New York. Marcella, who did know of Rose's existence, said that her husband swore he had never asked Ruth Rose to marry him. She added that after their marriage, they would occasionally see Rose at the ballet, and she would invariably glare at the new "Mrs." Corvino.

Becoming a U.S. Citizen

When Corvino entered the United States for the first time in June 1941, he was given a six-month visa. In the following years, he filed many applications to extend his stay, first through the Jooss company and then through the Ballet Russe. The back of Corvino's army induction orders described him as a "non-declarant alien" who had been administered the oath of service and obedience.

At the end of World War II, via the Second War Powers Act, the U.S. government offered the opportunity to the 122 aliens serving in the armed forces to obtain quick American citizenship, eliminating the normal two-year period of residence or waiting, and permitting naturalization to take place outside of the United States. But the Second War Powers Act expired on December 31, 1946, and Corvino either did not know of it or, more likely, was too involved with his court-martial and imprisonment. Thus it was not until 1949, at which time he had been back in the United States for the required two-year residency period, that Corvino applied for citizenship. He left the country, as was required, traveling to Toronto to meet with American INS agents and have the required documents signed and stamped. Afterward, he returned to New York by train and officially became a U.S. citizen on November 15, 1951.

Early Photos
(1800s–1961)

1. Alfredo Alfonso Corvino Sr.
photographer unknown, courtesy of the Corvino archives

2. Margarita (Julia) Dolce
photographer unknown, courtesy of the Corvino archives

3. Alfredo Corvino, circa 1919, "The violin was waiting for me before I was born"
photo by Fotografia Dolce, courtesy of the Corvino archives

4. Margarita Corvino, age five
photographer unknown, courtesy of the Corvino archives

5. Corvino *(left)* practices his boxing in Montevideo, circa 1932
photographer unknown, courtesy of the Corvino archives

6. Corvino rowing in Montevideo, circa 1933
photographer unknown, courtesy of the Corvino archives

7. Corvino in Montevideo, circa 1935
photographer unknown, courtesy of the Corvino archives

59

8. Corvino and Pepita Álvarez in Alberto Pouyanne's *La Isla de los Ceibos*, circa 1937
photographer unknown, courtesy of the Corvino archives

9. Corvino *(right)* in the Ballets Jooss production of *The Green Table*, 1940
photographer unknown, courtesy of the Corvino archives

10. Corvino in the leading role of the farm lad in the Ballet Russe de Monte Carlo production of Michel Fokine's *Igrouchki*, at City Center, New York City, circa 1943–44

photo by Marcella Rubin, courtesy of the Corvino archives

11. Ballet Russe de Monte Carlo production of Agnes de Mille's *Rodeo*, circa 1943–44. Corvino is far left.

photographer unknown, courtesy of the Corvino archives

12. Corvino in Ballet Russe de Monte
Carlo production of Pilar López's
Cuckold's Fair, circa 1944
  *photographer unknown, photo courtesy
  of the Corvino archives*

13. Ballet Russe de Monte Carlo production of Léonide Massine's *Gaîté
Parisienne* at City Center Theater, New York City, circa 1943–44. Corvino is the
waiter on the left.
  photo by Marcella Rubin, courtesy of the Corvino archives

14. Corvino on a break during Ballet Russe de Monte Carlo rehearsal at City Center studios, New York City, circa 1943

photo by Philip Rubin, courtesy of the Corvino archives

15. Marcella Rubin on the job as a young photographer, circa 1943–44

photographer unknown, courtesy of the Corvino archives

16. Pvt. Corvino in Germany, circa 1946
photographer unknown, courtesy of the Corvino archives

17. Entertainment specialist Corvino strikes a pose, Germany, circa 1946
photographer unknown, courtesy of the Corvino archives

18. Pvt. Corvino shows off his newly acquired skiing prowess in Switzerland, circa 1946
photographer unknown, courtesy of the Corvino archives

19. Alfredo Corvino and Marcella Rubin at their wedding, Long Island, NY, 1947

photographer unknown, courtesy of the Corvino archives

20. Corvino with Marcella and Andra, Brooklyn, NY, 1948

photographer unknown, courtesy of the Corvino archives

21. Marcella, Andra, and Ernesta, Brooklyn, NY, 1953

photographer unknown, courtesy of the Corvino archives

22. The Corvino family, Brooklyn, NY, 1961

photographer unknown, courtesy of the Corvino archives

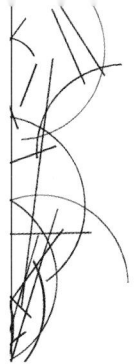

Chapter 4

MARCELLA RUBIN

Marcella Rubenstein was born August 12, 1918, in the Bronx, New York, the first child of Isabel Iskowitz Rubenstein and Joseph Rubenstein. Sometime before she entered school, her father changed and shortened the family name to Rubin. Her parents, married a year at the time of her birth, both grew up on the Lower East Side of Manhattan and had gone to the same schools. They were proud of their childhood friendship with the composer George Gershwin, a neighborhood boy made good.

The Jewish Immigrant Experience on the Lower East Side

Isabel and Joseph were part of the third-largest wave of Jewish immigration to the United States, which took place between 1881 and 1924. Although there were Irish and Italians among the 5,000 immigrants who were arriving at Ellis Island daily during this period, the majority of the newcomers to the Lower East Side were Yiddish-speaking Jews. They were escaping the pogroms—anti-Semitic rampages against entire towns and villages that left death and destruction in their wake—perpetuated by the czar's government in Russia, Poland, Romania, and Hungary.

The Jewish immigrants mostly lived in tenement houses—by definition any building inhabited by three or more families. Tenements had proliferated in this section of southeast Manhattan beginning in the mid-nineteenth century because the thousands upon thousands of new arrivals to the city needed inexpensive housing. By 1910, Manhattan had 2,500 six-story walkups that fit this description. Marcella's grandparents were lucky enough to arrive at a time when the law required indoor plumbing, toilets, and at least minimal ventilation. In the previous century, when the outhouses and the central water pump were next to each other in the tiny backyard that often became a pool of mud, outbreaks of disease were frequent and deadly.

This meant that each apartment, with approximately 325 square feet of living space, had running water, and every floor (usually containing four apartments) had two shared toilets in the hall. Each family dwelling had a tiny, doorless bedroom, into which a double bed barely fit, a kitchen that was the center of family life, and a small parlor that doubled as a second bedroom for family and boarders. There were often up to ten people living in one apartment, with one window in the living room and one in the bedroom that opened onto an airless shaft. Privacy was an unfamiliar luxury.

The narrow streets below the cramped, airless, and often unsanitary apartments were equally crowded, noisy, and pungent, containing jostling pushcarts selling everything from socks and pots and pans to raw vegetables and hot sweet potatoes. There were also small shops, most a few steps below street level. The street was teeming with vendors, adults, and children, many going to work in the stifling, crowded sweatshops that produced clothing. Laundry hanging to dry on lines filled every bit of available air space between the buildings.

Supporting a Family with Needle and Thread

Joseph Rubin had emigrated from Russia with his family when he was five. Isabel Iskowitz was nine when her mother brought her and her three siblings to New York in 1907. Isabel's mother arrived from Romania with only her children because her husband, a retired calvary officer, had received a homestead in Saskatchewan from the Canadian government, which he farmed for seven years. Isabel's mother, a highly urban creature, refused to spend her life on a farm or even to visit Canada, so, using her own earnings from her dressmaking establishment in Romania, she brought her family to the United States instead. Her husband sold the farm as soon as it officially became his and joined his family in New York City, where Isabel's mother had opened a neighborhood grocery store. Later, she returned to dressmaking.

Isabel Iskowitz had been called Miriam at birth, but when she contracted a serious childhood illness, her parents changed her name to Sophie so that "the angel of death would not find her." When she registered for school in New York City, her teacher said she looked like an Isabel, and this third name stuck. She remained Isabel for the rest of her life. Following in her mother's footsteps, she was working in the needle trades when she married Joseph, who was a shipping clerk. They had three children: Marcella, Philip (b. 1922), and Carryl (b. 1930). Joseph's modest earnings could have supported the family, but he was a compulsive gambler. His addiction, which used up most of his earnings, was fed at the local poolroom, where the object of the bet varied but was usually horses.

Isabel provided the family's main financial support. At times, she had her own dressmaking shop, on other occasions she worked as a seamstress for different employers. The family moved frequently: from the Bronx to Yonkers, Tarrytown, Manhattan, and finally Brooklyn, where they stayed. In retrospect, Marcella felt that her mother, who was socially ambitious, was attempting to move upward by making a commission on the sale of their home each time they moved. In Brooklyn, they started off in a loft, the front half of which was a small millinery factory that Isabel and Joseph started, and the rear their living quarters. Their final home, a house on East 7th Street near Kings Highway, was preceded by many rented apartments and loft domiciles in Brooklyn. Some of these moves were necessitated by an inability to pay the rent. When the Rubin family house on East 7th Street was purchased, Marcella paid a portion of the cost.

Marcella attended P.S. 153 in Brooklyn and Abraham Lincoln High School, graduating in 1932, just before she turned fifteen. An avid reader, she excelled in school and had skipped several grades.

Although her teachers urged this bright, inquisitive, and creative young woman to go to college, her parents needed her to work in their millinery business.

In that first loft in Brooklyn, the Rubins had started making inexpensive hats by hand, selling them to catalogue houses such as J.C. Penny, Sears Roebuck, and Montgomery Ward. They purchased pre-made hat forms—flimsy in their basic skeletal shapes—created a solid crown to cover the head, and then draped material around it and, sometimes, the brim. Little in the way of machinery was needed, and they employed anywhere from six to sixteen people, with Isabel overseeing the creation and Joseph the shipping. Marcella went directly from high school to making these hats and was given no choice in the matter. Naturally talented, she quickly progressed from copying an existing design to creating her own. She recalled hand sewing very inexpensive little hats that took a couple of minutes to make and were sold for about two dollars a dozen. "I was born with a needle in my hand," she said. "I don't remember learning."

In 1936, when she was eighteen, Marcella left the Rubin home to marry Bob Adler. The couple moved to Akron, Ohio. She was a beautiful young woman, and he was completely smitten with her. Marcella later admitted that she had entered into this marriage because it was her only way of escaping her parents. One of the jobs she had in Akron was as a hostess in a restaurant. She had applied for a waitressing job but was so thin—she weighed eighty-five pounds—that they considered her too frail to carry a tray. During this time, she also drove an emergency medical truck. Although Marcella divorced and returned to her parents eight years later, in 1944, it was with a stronger sense of herself and a determination to do at least some things her way.

Upon her return to New York, Marcella and her parents together opened a new millinery business in Brooklyn. In a retail store in front, called Hats by Marcella, they sold expensive custom-designed hats, and in a small factory in the back, they produced wholesale, inexpensive ones. She and her mother designed the retail hats, and her father ran the wholesale business. If Joseph became excessively busy in the factory, the two women would leave the shop and come back and help out.

Strained Family Relations

Commenting on her grandparents after her mother's death, Andra Corvino said that Marcella felt they had long taken advantage of her. They were young and naïve when she was born, and a baby only compounded Joseph's perennial difficulties in paying the rent. As Marcella was growing up, her parents often made fun of her, calling her fat and stupid. They were short-tempered and punished her frequently. They lacked the emotional capacity or ability to nurture her, yet she always took care of them, at first because they forced her to and then because she felt an obligation to do so. Yet Marcella continued to seek their approval right up until their deaths. Although Andra remembers that her grandmother could be blunt and unkind, Ernesta, four years her junior and often left in her grandmother's care, says she was also fun-loving and insightful.

Isabel Rubin decided that Phil, her only son, would go to college. An unmotivated underachiever who was nevertheless very intelligent and artistic, he attended Kent State University while Marcella was living in Akron. He was a "jack of all trades" until he took up photography, which became his profession. Phil eventually married a domineering woman named Dorothy Gordon, the sister of a choreographer, Marvin Gordon, who had his own dance company. According to Andra, Dorothy went rampaging through the house after Isabel's death in 1968, demanding certain of her personal items. This unpleasant and upsetting scene opened a permanent rift in the relationship between Phil and Marcella. It had been a close one in their early adulthood but had become strained and more distant following his marriage.

Carryl, the baby of the Rubin family and twelve years younger than Marcella, was constantly told by her parents that she was "an accident." She was a serious ballet student, and at one time she studied at the Ballet Arts studio in Carnegie Hall. She married three times. Her first husband, Steve, a housing authority officer, once threatened her with his service gun. The marriage lasted only four years. Her second husband, Jim, an older divorcé with a family, worked for Planned Parenthood. Her third husband, Sam, was in the Ben Franklin art business. Despite their shared interests in dance, Marcella and Carryl were estranged for most of their adult lives. When they were younger, however, Marcella felt very maternal toward her younger sister, and she said that when she first met Alfredo she considered him as a possible match for her sister, not herself.

Finding Enchantment at the Russian Tea Room

Marcella was a balletomane long before she met Alfredo. As a very young child, she took dance and decorum lessons at a time when her parents, who had all the upwardly mobile aspirations of new immigrants, could still afford them. Her redheaded aunt Fanny, one of her mother's sisters, was very theatrical and gave dance classes, although she herself had probably never taken any.

Marcella studied at a theater school on Broadway and 83rd Street, where a three-hour class for children was offered on Saturday mornings. This class included dance, recitation, and singing, with monthly recitals. Marcella also studied ballet with a teacher named Sidonia Menkes.

In addition, Marcella studied with a dance teacher who had trained in Isadora Duncan's technique—a young woman who lived on Gramercy Park and who created a large dance space in her house by opening the connecting doors between the rooms of the first floor. The students all wore chiffon tunics and were allowed to express themselves by dancing with freedom and abandon. This approach was very popular in the physical education of girls in the 1920s. Spurred by the aesthetics of Duncan, which by this time had become well-known in America, it was part of the prevailing cultural climate that heralded the emancipation of women—including freedom from torturous corsets, freedom to wear short skirts and bobbed hair, freedom to be athletic and physically active, freedom to smoke and drink, and the freedom to vote. Some dance teachers were Duncan-trained, others merely

Duncan-inspired, but legions of middle-class girls were "becoming" butterflies or raindrops in dance classes nationwide. Unfortunately for Marcella, her dance lessons ceased at an early age.

When she returned to Brooklyn from her temporary, self-imposed exile in Akron, Marcella's creative side found an outlet not only in designing hats but also in assisting her brother in his photography career. With her keen visual perception, she was soon developing her own aesthetic vision and was taking photographs herself. Meanwhile, she went to the ballet all the time and was thoroughly familiar with the repertoire of the Ballet Russe de Monte Carlo. "I stumbled into the Russian Tea Room one day to get out of the rain. I did not know that this was the place all the ballet people went [to] after the performance," she later recalled.

The Russian Tea Room, at 150 West 57th Street in Manhattan, was physically and politically to the left of Carnegie Hall, the mecca of classical music. Opened by Russian émigrés in 1927, it was, for decades, the center of what later became known as power lunches, Sunday brunch, and the place to see and be seen at dinner and after performances—a glittering, effervescent, and stimulating convergence of dancers, musicians, artists, actors, and writers. Re-creating an atmosphere of czarist Russian grandeur, the red and green room, filled with shining samovars, retained its Christmas decorations year-round and was always bathed in a golden light. The red leather banquets that lined the green lacquered walls were reserved for famous people only. Brusque waiters, dressed in red Russian-style uniforms, served red cabbage, borscht, blintzes, blinis with caviar, beef stroganoff, and the Tea Room's famous drink, the Moscow Mule, a mixture of vodka and ginger beer.

Yet the Russian Tea Room was also a place frequented by lesser-known creative artists and by Russian and Polish immigrants who could only afford cookies and tea sweetened with jam to accompany their earnest and spirited discussions. On Saturday afternoons, these intellectually rich patrons of modest means were joined by young ballet students who came with their mothers or grandmothers for an after-class lunch.

Drawn in by this enchanted and enchanting atmosphere, Marcella returned to the Russian Tea Room again and again, gradually becoming acquainted with the dancers and their fans and joining the frenetic table-hopping activity. They would sit and gossip, eat a bite, and then move to another table and repeat the process. Marcella never figured out how the waiters knew to whom to give the check. Sometimes she went for brunch and would encounter Alexandra Danilova and her husband. Sometimes, she dined with not only dancers from the Ballet Russe and Ballet Theatre but also the Russian Jewish acting group that included Joseph Buloff and Eli Wallach.

For Marcella, it was "a home away from home." Her best friend, Shirley Goldwater, a former dancer who eventually wrote for *Dance Magazine*, often accompanied her. Sometimes Marcella, Phil, and Isabel went to the ballet with Goldwater and her mother, and afterward they all trouped over to the Russian Tea Room together. Marcella thrived in this exuberant atmosphere with its resemblance to eastern European Jewish intellectual gatherings.

Alfredo Corvino, on the occasions he was there, observed this golden hive of activity and silently absorbed it all. Most particularly, his eye was drawn and captured by Marcella Rubin.

The First Meeting and Slow Courtship

By now, Marcella knew and was known by most of the ballet dancers who frequented the Russian Tea Room. She had already seen Alfredo perform several times before they first met. One day in 1943, Goldwater hired Phil Rubin to take some photographs for *Dance Magazine*, and Marcella served as his assistant on this assignment. Marcella never revealed whether or not her brother actually paid her for her help, but monetary recompense was irrelevant to her in this particular case.

Marcella adored the dance world atmosphere. She and Phil went to City Center to photograph a Ballet Russe rehearsal of *The Red Poppy*, *Le Bourgeois Gentilhomme*, and *Rodeo*. It was at this shoot that Marcella and Alfredo were formally introduced. Alfredo was very friendly with Phil, telling him about all the boys in the company who were in love with his sister. When Phil told Marcella this, she said, "That doesn't sound quite right to me. I know a few of them are in love with each other, and the ones who might look at a woman already have one."

Years later, Alfredo admitted to Marcella that, in paying her this compliment via her brother, he had just been fishing for more information about her. At first he thought Phil was Marcella's boyfriend or fiancé. He thought it was strange that these "Anglo-Saxon types" could be so cool and dispassionate in such a presumably intimate, loving relationship. Disabused of his misconceptions about Phil and Marcella's true relationship, Corvino started coming to the Russian Tea Room in the evenings. He even met Marcella's mother several times. It was Isabel who invited him to Brooklyn for a home-cooked meal, and Corvino not only enjoyed the meal but was also delighted by the spaciousness of the Rubin house. By this time, Marcella was beginning to think of Corvino as a possible suitor for her sister. What Isabel thought about Corvino's possible future within the family—and to whom he would become attached—is unknown.

Meanwhile, Corvino continued dancing, and Marcella was busy with her hat-making business in Brooklyn, assisting her brother with his photography, and frequenting the Russian Tea Room after ballet performances. She also took backstage photos on her own. Frederic Franklin, who was then in his first year as ballet master, wanted someone to photograph the corps dancers so that he could see what they were doing when he was performing as a soloist in front of them. According to Marcella, Franklin asked her, rather than Phil, to take on this assignment because he didn't consider it a professional job but just a favor between friends. Marcella accepted because, as she said, "I kind of liked the idea of being able to go to the theater every night—to rush out of the storm, grab the subway, and have something to do."

It was at this point that Corvino was drafted by the U.S. Army, a sudden development that required him to think and act quickly before departing for basic training. His belongings had been stored in the basement of the Park Savoy Hotel, and he telephoned Marcella to ask if she would be willing to store them for him in her house in Brooklyn. He also asked her to collect the money the Ballet Russe owed him, gave her his bankbook and power of attorney, and asked her to deposit whatever checks he might mail to her. Finally, he asked her to send his mother a certain amount of money from his account each month.

The Rubins considered Corvino a family friend at this point. On one of his furloughs home from Florida, he showed up unannounced in Brooklyn. Isabel told him Marcella was not home; she had gone to a performance of Ballet Theatre to see the great Cuban ballerina Alicia Alonso dance *Giselle* for the first time in New York. Marcella had waited too long to purchase a ticket for a decent seat and had just wiggled into a good standing room spot and was waiting expectantly for the curtain to go up on act II when she felt someone rubbing her back. She turned around to see a soldier "very brown, very plump, with a big black mustache." Thinking she was speaking to a stranger, she said, "I'm sorry, but I was here first." As soon as the stranger smiled, however, Marcella recognized him as Alfredo.

This was the night when she first realized Corvino's romantic interest in her, but she had a few love interests of her own and did not want to get overly involved with a neophyte dancer and recently drafted soldier. She was tired of being poor and had begun dating older men with a little money. But that night she took a fresh look at Corvino and thought, "He's not too bad." She was also impressed by the fact that, on his meager salary from Ballet Russe, he fed and clothed himself, sent his mother money, and managed to save more than $4,000.

A spark had been kindled, and Marcella and Alfredo corresponded regularly while he was overseas. After he was discharged from the army, he came immediately to Brooklyn to collect his belongings and see Marcella. He was determined to find a place to live in Manhattan. The fledgling couple started seeing each other with growing frequency and intensity.

Only Marcella's letters to Corvino remain from their wartime correspondence. At the end, they were unambiguous love letters. He had also been writing to Ruth Rose, as the papers concerning the court martial procedure indicated. Whether or not Corvino saw Rose after his return is unknown. He did tell Marcella about her, saying that he had "played around a bit," but he swore that he had never proposed marriage, although Rose had told everyone they were engaged.

Marriage and a Solid, Enduring Love

Alfredo and Marcella were married on June 28, 1947, at a friend's home on Long Island, by a judge who was a family relation. For some reason, their marriage certificate is dated July 19, 1947.

With the exception of his dalliance with Ruth Rose, Corvino did not tell Marcella about any of his past affairs, and she told him that she was not interested in knowing about them. He, in turn, never, throughout their fifty-seven years of marriage, asked her about her divorce, and they never even discussed their own relationship with each other. He knew that Marcella had inquired about him a great deal before she made her decision to get fully involved. He recognized that she had taken a chance on him. "She put her eyes on me," he said with a grin when speaking, after her death, of their courtship. Once married, Corvino rested secure in the knowledge that Marcella was entirely devoted to him. He acknowledged her quality of leadership, admitting that she was the "guiding light" in their marriage, home, and life.

Before their wedding, Corvino told Marcella that he was "married" to the ballet and asked her to promise him that she would never interfere with any aspect of his career in dance. Marcella made and kept that promise, which was often difficult and frustrating. Corvino was both an intensely focused workaholic and an extremely private person who did not often or easily reveal his emotions. Marcella once told someone that the door was always open for Alfredo, and he could come and go as he wished. Although both Alfredo and Marcella were warm, loving individuals, neither was physically demonstrative toward the other, at least not in public. Yet in their last year together, he could often be observed rubbing her arm very gently as they sat side by side at their round dining table at their home on 50th Street.

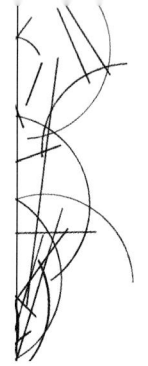

Chapter 5

TRANSITIONS: A DANCER
BECOMES A TEACHER

When he was honorably discharged from the army on March 6, 1947, Corvino returned to a country dramatically altered by both its experience of war and its enjoyment of victory.

Women, who had left the home to work in the defense and war industries, did not always want to return to a homemaker role, and when they did, it was with a different attitude and a stronger sense of self. Many of the men now studying under the G.I. Bill were older college students who had never considered higher education in the pre-war years. African Americans, though almost a decade away from the advent of the civil rights movement, were already beginning to organize themselves and mobilize toward their goals. An early step in this slow march toward racial equality was Jackie Robinson's debut with the Brooklyn Dodgers in 1947, when he became the first African American to play on a major league baseball team, opening the door a crack to eventual full integration of the league (not to mention other major professional and college sports).

Even as one sector of American society was beginning to embrace inclusion, thereby fulfilling the long unrealized promise of the country's founding principles, some of the nation's leaders were busy undermining the Constitution and attacking—and in some cases destroying—innocent and law-abiding citizens. Wisconsin senator Eugene McCarthy, head of the Un-American Activities Committee, which sought to cleanse America of any and all "subversive" communists, was spreading fear throughout the performing arts and media industries. Writers, dancers, actors, musicians, and filmmakers with left-leaning sympathies and/or a history of membership in socialist or communist political parties were blacklisted for refusing to testify before the committee or giving up the names of supposed Communist Party members and sympathizers. Ten people on the Hollywood Black List were imprisoned for refusing to testify before Congress.

Despite the intolerance, political repression, and fear growing within the United States, outwardly the country dominated the international stage as the most powerful and prosperous of the world powers in the devastating wake of World War II. It emerged from the war stronger, more productive, and more confident than it had entered, something that could not be said even of the other victorious Allied powers. In the immediate postwar years, the United States was the only country in the world with both a functioning political system and the ability to maintain its high economic productivity, putting it in a position to strongly influence—and in some cases dictate—world events. This newfound strength, confidence, and influence could be put to good ends, such as the implementation of the Marshall Plan in 1947, which provided economic aid to often impoverished, starving, and shattered European countries suffering in the devastating aftermath of war.

On Broadway, Tennessee Williams won a Pulitzer Prize for *A Streetcar Named Desire*. Musicals of 1947 included *High Button Shoes*, with choreography by Jerome Robbins, and *Brigadoon*, choreographed by Agnes de Mille. The Dramatists Guild and Actors Equity organized the Experimental Theatre to create new ideas and a viable "Off Broadway" theater culture. As a result, small theaters, many in Greenwich Village, became more active, both creatively and financially. At this same time, television started to enter homes, undermining live theater, yet also exposing millions of Americans to some form of dance and drama, in many cases for the first time in their lives.

In dance, which had risen in popularity during the war years, Ballet Theatre and the Ballet Russe were both presenting works by new choreographers. Modern dance was producing a new generation of artists, including José Limón, the Mexican American who had performed with Doris Humphrey and Charles Weidman and who was to become one of America's leading male dancers and choreographers.

Ballet Arts

How aware the thirty-one-year-old Corvino was of this dynamic swirl of events in the early postwar period is unknown, but having been discharged from the army, he quickly started creating a new postwar life for himself and began to refashion his dance career. As soon as he was free of his responsibilities to the armed forces, Pfc. Corvino took advantage of the ensuing rights he had earned. One of these was the G.I. Bill of Rights—officially referred to as the Serviceman's Readjustment Act of 1944—which allowed veterans to enroll in classes for vocational as well as college training. Under the aegis of the American Theatre Wing, which administered the program, Corvino received money to study while he sorted out his life, plotted his career, and decided what to do next to further both.

He began his quest at Ballet Arts, the famous Studio 61. It was organizationally part of Carnegie Hall, the venerable music theater on West 57th Street, but it was housed in a separate building, with its own entrance and an elevator manned by a uniformed employee. The building contained numerous teaching studios for the performing arts, as well as small apartments where members of the different theatrical professions lived.

One took the elevator to 6-8, a combined floor, turned right, and walked up a few stairs before coming to a double door marked "Studio 61." The left side said Nimura Studio, and the right Ballet Arts. This joint enterprise was presided over by Virginia Lee, the large, dominating school director (and former dancer). Lee had met the dancer Yeichi Nimura in the 1930s, when, at one point, they together ran the studio for a woman named Alys Bentley. When World War II broke out, Lee was managing the European performances of Nimura and his partner Lisan Kay. When Lee and Nimura returned to the United States in 1939, they took over Bentley's studio, with Nimura serving as codirector.

At different times, teachers at Ballet Arts included Vera Fokina (Michel Fokine's wife), Bronislava Nijinska, Vera Nemchinova, Vladimir Dokoudovsky, and Lisan Kay. Famous pupils who studied there in the 1940s included Nana Gollner, Paul Petroff, James Starbuck, and Sono

Osato from the Ballet Russe; Bambi Linn, Allyn McLerie, Gemze de Lappe, and Rod Alexander from Broadway; and Diana Adams from Ballet Theatre and, later, the New York City Ballet. Agnes de Mille rehearsed *Rodeo* there. At one point, it was even possible to witness a pregnant de Mille teaching a class that included a lanky, dark-haired Jerome Robbins, who had already choreographed the ballet *Fancy Free*, as well as several Broadway productions.

Corvino took class there with Edward Caton and Antony Tudor for a total of seven and a half hours a week. Caton was born in Russia and studied in Moscow and St. Petersburg as a private pupil of Agrippina Vaganova, the famous ballet pedagogue. He danced with Pavlova and with the Mordkin Ballet and was a charter member of Ballet Theatre. He was ballet master with the Ballet Russe in 1943 and, later, with Ballet Theatre. He was a very popular teacher.

Antony Tudor (1908–1987) was born in England, where he studied with Marie Rambert, the Dalcroze- and Cecchetti-trained teacher who had taught and mentored Nijinsky and was known for fostering chore-ographers. Later, Tudor also studied with Pearl Argyle and Margaret Craske. He joined Ballet Rambert in 1930 as a dancer and assistant to Rambert. Soon after, he began choreographing and produced so many successful ballets that, in 1940, Ballet Theatre invited him to join as one of its initial choreographers. He moved to New York that year and remained there ever after (with occasional teaching stints in California and Europe), becoming one of the foremost choreographers of the twentieth century. Tudor was cognizant of and embraced the artistic innovations of Kurt Jooss. Tudor's use of dramatic gesture to define a character, along with his psychological insight into human motivation and the suffering of ordinary people, affected not only audiences but other choreographers as well. His choreography sought to reveal what often lies buried in human interactions. Tudor once said that if some-one did not understand exactly what his ballets meant, he had failed as a creator.

Corvino also studied at Ballet Arts with Yeichi Nimura, who had trained in martial arts in his native Japan before studying ballet, modern, and Spanish classical dance in the United States. Nimura's technique was labeled "plastique" in the circular describing his classes.

Clothed in billowing pants, bare-chested, his black hair slicked back, he moved in a fluid, feline fashion that was mesmerizing.

Another important and influential teacher at Ballet Arts was Margaret Craske (1892–1990). This English dancer, choreographer, and teacher was an exponent of the technique of Enrico Cecchetti, with whom she studied for five years in London. She danced with the Diaghilev Ballets Russes and later opened a school in London, where not only Tudor but also the ballerina Margot Fonteyn and the chore-ographers Frederick Ashton and Agnes de Mille were her pupils. She spent seven years in India with the guru Meher Baba before Ballet Theatre invited her to become ballet mistress in 1946. Her teaching was known for its simplicity, its elegance, the flow of the upper body, and her precise and exacting methods. Although Corvino did not study with her at Ballet Arts, he would later have contact with her at the Metropolitan Opera House and at Juilliard.

During his time at Ballet Arts, Corvino enrolled in a course in Labanotation, wishing to learn more about the anatomical, spatial, and temporal aspects of Laban's method of writing dance. He sought this knowledge in order to balance the qualitative aspects of Laban's method that he had learned in the Jooss company. The course's instructor, Lucy Venable, was a young dancer who had studied with Doris Humphrey and José Limón, and later performed with the Limón company and the Merry-Go-Rounders.

The Merry-Go-Rounders was a repertory group founded in 1952 and based at the 92nd Street Young Men's-Young Women's Hebrew Association (more popularly referred to as the 92nd Street Y). It offered performances for children, while simultaneously giving professional experience to young dancers. The company was unique in the sense that, in accordance with the philosophy of the 92nd Street Y, it aimed to simultaneously educate children about the art of dance and teach them something important about Jewish heritage in a multicultural world.

Still actively involved in dance notation following her retirement from Ohio State University in 1992, Venable remembers nothing about Corvino's notation abilities but does recall that they both took drumming classes together at Katherine Dunham's school, which they found difficult and painful to their hands. Dunham was a Chicago-born dancer, choreographer, and anthropologist who had developed a technique that combined ballet and Caribbean dance, especially African-influenced Haitian dance. She was one of the pioneers of black concert dance. Her school in New York, established in 1945, had a dance and theater division, a department of cultural studies, and the Institute for Caribbean Research.

Teaching at the Shurman School and the Olga Tarassova School

At this same time, Corvino started teaching at the Shurman School, owned and operated by Sunya Shurman, at Studio 843 Carnegie Hall, just upstairs from Ballet Arts. Corvino had previously taken a class there with Anna Istomina, along with some other dancers from the Ballet Russe, before he went into the army. Istomina, née Audree Thomas, was a Canadian dancer with great technical skill. Corvino knew her from the Ballet Russe. Following the war, Istomina was still teaching at the Shurman School and was pregnant. When she became ill during the pregnancy, Corvino was asked to take over her class. Here he taught what he called "Jooss-influenced" classes. He was encouraged in this by Shurman, who had studied with the German modern dancer Harald Kreutzberg, danced on Broadway and in the Ziegfeld Follies, and claimed to have had experience in all aspects of performance.

This was Corvino's official teaching debut, although he had taught children in Uruguay and offered informal instruction for some of his Jooss, Ballet Russe, and Soldier Show Workshop colleagues. Shortly after being given Istomina's class, he left the Shurman School to join the Olga Tarassova School on 54th Street near Sixth Avenue. Tarassova, a Russian-born dancer, was a friend of Anatole Vilzak's, who had arranged for Tarassova and Corvino to meet. In discussing his career, Corvino never indicated why he left the Shurman School, but it seems likely that Tarassova's classical approach would have felt more comfortable to him than Shurman's eclectic approach to dance training.

Just before Christmas 1947, Corvino went to work at Radio City Music Hall, where Margaret Sandy was the ballet mistress and Genia Melnichenko, also known as Genia Melikova, a former soloist with Ballet Theatre who had been a pupil of Vilzak's, was the leading dancer. Corvino said he performed in four shows a day for eleven weeks at Radio City, teaching one class a day at Tarassova's between shows. A program from Radio City Music Hall in Corvino's archives for the week beginning May 6, 1948, lists him as one of the featured dancers.

The Metropolitan Opera Ballet

In the autumn of 1947, Corvino auditioned once more for the Metropolitan Opera Ballet, which he had turned down five years earlier in favor of the Ballet Russe. According to Corvino, he was accepted, but due to a mix-up, another dancer received the contract. It was not until November 29, 1948, therefore, that Alfredo Corvino began four weeks of rehearsal, at $35 per week, as a member of the Met Ballet (as it was known by dance insiders). Following the rehearsal period, Corvino performed for twelve weeks at $60 per week. He went on tour from March 21, 1949, through May 22, at a salary of $102 per week.

The following year, the Met Ballet season, which paid $60 per week, was approximately eighteen weeks long, again with four weeks of rehearsal at $35 per week. By the 1952–53 season, which ran for twenty-two weeks, with six weeks of rehearsal, the pay was $75 per week for performances and $40 per week for rehearsals. Corvino left the company after the 1953–54 season, giving as his reason the fact that when he returned from one six-week tour, his second daughter, the one-year-old Ernesta, screamed, apparently with fear, when she saw what she took to be a stranger.

While Corvino danced with the Met, he initially took class with Boris Romanov, who was the ballet master and choreographer for the

84

company. This alumnus of Diaghilev's Ballets Russes taught a very lyrical class. Corvino never forgot that when class was going well, Romanov would exclaim "Coca Cola!" as a vocal seal of approval. Starting in 1949, Corvino danced solos, duets, and trios in Met productions of *Carmen* (Bizet), *The Marriage of Figaro* (Mozart), *Mignon* (Thomas), and *Samson and Delilah* (Saint-Saëns). When Rudolf Bing was appointed general manager of the Metropolitan Opera in 1950, he wanted Ballet Theatre and Lucia Chase, its artistic director, to take over the Met's ballet school and company, which they did for the 1949–50 season. Antony Tudor became director of the school and the company, and Margaret Craske served as ballet mistress of the company and joined the school faculty. Most of the Met Ballet dancers were fired, with members of Ballet Theatre replacing them, but Tudor remembered Corvino from Ballet Arts and kept him on.

June Evans, who had studied with Craske and Tudor at Ballet Arts and performed in the corps de ballet at Radio City Music Hall, danced with the Met Ballet company during the 1950–51 season. She met Corvino at a rehearsal for the act II waltz in *Die Fledermaus* (Strauss Jr.). She was tall, and she took one look at this short, muscular man who was to be her partner and decided he was the worst possible match for her. She was prepared to go crying to Craske. But Evans soon realized that this gentle, respectful, stable dancer was actually one of the best partners possible, capable of lifting with ease any ballerina of any size. She also remembers company class with Tudor, who could be awful to everyone but never scolded Corvino.

Alexander Gavrilov, another Russian who had danced with Diaghilev, was the first ballet master of Ballet Theatre. At Tudor's request, he held the same position at the Met Ballet after Tudor took over. Corvino always listed him as one of his teachers. Gavrilov immediately formed a small company within the company, using nine members of the Met Ballet, including Corvino, in a work called *Ballet Carnival*. It consisted of six short dances to composers ranging from Beethoven to Shostakovitch, and he choreographed and directed it with the full backing of the opera administration. Credited simply as "Members of the Metropolitan Ballet," they performed at the Newport Music Festival in Newport, Rhode Island, in September

1949. Based on a letter in the Corvino archives written by Gavrilov and dated July 29, 1949, they probably toured extensively in New England that summer.

The following year, this elite group returned to the festival, but this time Tilda Morse and Alfredo Corvino were the featured dancers. There was no mention of Gavrilov for these performances, and Morse was listed as producer and director. Morse was a soloist at the Met, where she and Corvino danced the "Bolero" in *Carmen* together. At Newport, the group performed in a work for four, called *Square Dance* (Raphling), in Fokine's *Le Spectre de la Rose*, and in *Suite of Four Dancers* (Ravel). They closed the first half of the program with the premiere of *Manhattan Moods* (Alter). The latter piece was said to be choreographed by Alfredo Corvino. The second half of the program mostly featured solos, with Corvino dancing the "Dance of the Ribbons" from *The Red Poppy*.

A review by Ruth Tripp in a local newspaper on September 17, 1950, noted that *Le Spectre de la Rose* gave the two dancers, Morse and Corvino, the finest opportunity of the evening to show their skill and was "superb." She found the ribbon dance a "breathtaking display of color" produced by the whipping ribbon that was "manipulated by Corvino with the utmost dexterity." Corvino's *Manhattan Moods* was deemed a "definite contribution to ballet literature" that included a sophisticated lady (Morse), a naïve maiden (Peggy Smithers, a soloist at the Met), and two men. The program did not list the dancers for this piece, so little else is known.

Corvino joined the American Guild of Musical Artists (AGMA) several years before he came to the Met (probably while he was with the Ballet Russe), and in August 1951, he was invited to serve for one year on the AGMA board of governors to fill out the term of someone who had resigned. The following year, he was elected to serve a three-year term. He enjoyed this "other world" of dance as he called it and was diligent in fulfilling his duties. In later years, he would bring the same earnest concentration and work ethic to the dance panel of the New York State Council on the Arts, on which he sat from 1988 to 1990.

Choreographer's Workshop and Other Important Performances

The Choreographer's Workshop was a pickup company of sorts, put together for a specific series of performances. It was codirected by the dancer, choreographer, and director Herbert Ross with visual artist and set designer John Ward. Ross started out performing on Broadway and went on to create works for Ballet Theatre, for his own company, and for several Broadway musicals. The former included the ballets *Caprichos* (Bartok), with sets by Ward, and *The Maids* (Milhaud). For Broadway, Ross choreographed *I Can Get It for You Wholesale* and a production of *Finian's Rainbow*. Ross was also very active in Hollywood as a director and choreographer, with *A Turning Point* being his most famous dance film. His first works were created for the Choreographer's Workshop.

Alice Green, whom Corvino knew from the Met Ballet, brought him into the Choreographer's Workshop—a group of seven dancers that initially performed at the 92nd Street Y in New York City, and then in Suffern (a Rockland County suburb of New York City) and at Jacob's Pillow in Massachusetts. The Pillow was a farm whose name was inspired by the biblical story about Jacob's vision of a stairway (or "ladder") leading to Heaven, dreamt as his head rested on a stone pillow. The zig-zagging road leading to the farm was said to resemble Jacob's ladder, and a flat boulder behind the farmhouse evoked Jacob's stone pillow. The farm was purchased by Ted Shawn in 1931. Two years later, Shawn established an all-male dance company and, eventually, an internationally recognized school and summer dance festival on the property.

Shawn had entered the American dance scene in 1914, when he became the partner of Ruth St. Denis. Their company, Denishawn, toured the world, and their eclectic school, Denishawn School of Dancing and Related Arts, greatly influenced the development of American modern dance and dancers. Shawn and St. Denis provided the training ground for Martha Graham, Doris Humphrey, Charles Weidman, and others.

Corvino recalled that at Jacob's Pillow, the dancers were put up in a barn, there was never enough food, and Ross and Shawn (who liked to be called "Papa Shawn" because of his role in American dance) argued continuously. He remembered two of Ross's works in particular: *The Black Cat* (Berg), based on a story by Edgar Allen Poe, and *Pierrot and the Moon* (Stravinsky), in which Corvino had to do a *relevé* in *arabesque* from a kneeling position. This meant he had to rise straight up on one leg while simultaneously lifting the other, a movement that required him to have intimate knowledge of his center of weight and how to keep it in constant motion, even when seemingly still. Tudor saw his performance in *Pierrot* and commented to Corvino that he never stopped moving, a complimentary observation that Corvino always treasured.

Corvino was to return to the 92nd Street Y from 1954 to 1956, when he taught a warm-up class for the Merry-Go-Rounders prior to rehearsal, replacing Robert Joffrey, the future choreographer and company director of the Joffrey Ballet. During the 1955–56 season, Corvino taught a daily class in advanced technique, Monday through Friday, from 1:00 PM to 2:30 PM. Naomi Jackson, in her book about the 92nd Street Y, *Converging Movements*, says it was a combination of performing experiences and Corvino's classes that were the most important factors in drawing talented young people to the company.

During the summer of 1952, Corvino drove his new, black 1951 Studebaker daily to the Jones Beach Theater on Long Island, where he danced in the Michael Todd production *A Night in Venice*. Set to the music of Johann Strauss, it had sets and costumes by Raoul Pene DuBois and was choreographed by James Nygren, assisted by Alice Green, who was probably responsible for recruiting Corvino to dance in it. Corvino remembered that Todd, a well-known theater and film producer who later married the actress Elizabeth Taylor, would bring the dancers sandwiches so they could work overtime, rehearsing on the outdoor stage on Zach's Bay in the blazing sun. They swam in the lagoon on breaks in order to cool off.

Among the dancers were Loren (Tex) Hightower, a Texan who danced on Broadway and with Ballet Theatre; Peter Deign, Corvino's friend from the Ballet Russe; Wilma Curley, who danced with the New

York City Ballet, in Jerome Robbins's Ballets: USA, and on Broadway, and restaged Robbins's ballets all over the world; and Cathryn Damon, who went on to become a star of the 1970s sitcom *Soap*.

Teaching at Jacob's Pillow and Elsewhere

Several years after he first performed at Jacob's Pillow, Corvino was invited by Ted Shawn to become a member of the summer faculty. In 1957, Corvino agreed to teach ten classes a week, five beginners and five advanced, for a period of three weeks. The total salary was $300, plus room and board for the entire Corvino family.

By then, the family had reached its full size, including Alfredo, Marcella, and their two daughters: Andra, born in 1948, and Ernesta, born in 1952. Corvino was encouraged to inform his New York students that they could take classes at $1.50 per session, and Shawn's contractual letter indicated that Jacob's Pillow would be happy to assist such students in finding cheap housing. Private lessons were permissible, with Corvino and Jacob's Pillow sharing the student fees fifty/fifty.

In 1958, Shawn wrote to Marcella, asking that she send him a wire, collect, indicating whether or not Corvino would again teach for the first three weeks in July. This time, though, the Pillow would pick up only half of the Corvinos' room and board. There was some confusion about Corvino's teaching plans because Shawn had initially asked Mattlyn Gavers, who had first declined and then changed her mind after Corvino was invited in her stead. When Corvino learned of this awkward situation, he graciously told Shawn to hire Gavers, who then said "no" again. Shawn thanked both the Corvinos profusely for their patience and understanding. Corvino did not teach at the Pillow in 1959 or 1960. A handwritten note addressed to Marcella and Alfredo, dated July 24, 1960, and signed "Papa Shawn," enclosed a clipping from a local newspaper and said, "We miss you already. Come back and see us now and then." The following summer, 1961, was Corvino's last at the Pillow.

According to Andra, those weeks at Jacob's Pillow were wonderful family holidays, with her grandmother and her mother's aunt and uncle joining them at the guesthouse, Brookside Lodge. She vividly remembers long drives through the Berkshire Mountains, enjoying the scenery.

Corvino's teaching credits over the years encompassed numerous programs, schools, and festivals throughout the United States, Europe, and Asia. Included among these were festivals in Hong Kong, Taipei, and Tokyo. He also taught at the Cloud Gate Dance Theatre in Taipei (1987), the New World School of the Arts in Miami (1988), and one semester as an adjunct at the State University of New York at Purchase (1987). He had guest teaching stints at the University of California at Long Beach, the Repertory Dance Theatre of Utah, and Philadanco in Philadelphia (1993).

In the early days of his teaching career, Corvino taught during the summers either in a rented studio at Showcase Studios on 56th Street and Eighth Avenue in Manhattan or in one at Dance Players on 48th Street and Sixth Avenue, where José Limón also taught. As a young child, Andra remembers spending hours at these two places, since Marcella always worked as the receptionist at the desk. One year, Andra told her mother about her new friend down the hall, Joe. Further investigation revealed that her new playmate was none other than José Limón. Many summers later, including those of 1989 and 1991, Corvino taught as part of the Limón Dance Workshop at SUNY-Purchase. For a number of years, he also taught for the Philadelphia Dance Guild.

Corvino's First Important Choreographic Efforts

The Philadelphia Dance Guild was formed in the mid-1950s, as a result of Eugene Ormandy's desire to have classical ballet dancers perform with the Philadelphia Orchestra. Ormandy, the Hungarian-born conductor, was the music director of the Philadelphia Orchestra for forty-two years.

The guild, a loose coalition of Philadelphia ballet teachers, invited Antony Tudor to come from New York City to teach three classes on Sundays. Tudor brought in Matlyn Gavers and Corvino, each of whom was scheduled to teach one Sunday a month, while Tudor taught two Sundays. But Corvino often covered Tudor's classes, driving himself down to Philadelphia and back. This went on for several years, and while Tudor created or set several works for Ormandy, including *Les Petits Riens* (Mozart) in 1956, Corvino choreographed a dance for the yearly cotillion presented by the black community of Philadelphia.

The guild, never a strong organization, slowly faded out of existence, but it nevertheless left a unique and important legacy. It gave many advanced black ballet dancers an opportunity to study with Tudor and Corvino in an integrated class. This was a rarity in Philadelphia at the time, where there was still a form of de facto segregation. Black dancers had to study with one of only two black ballet teachers in the city, Marion Cuyjet or Sydney King, both of whom sent their students to the guild's Sunday classes.

Corvino never thought of these students in terms of skin color but rather in terms of talent and potential. He retained memories of Joan Myers Brown, a student of both King's and Cuyjet's, who went on to form her own highly successful school and company, Philadanco; John Jones, who later studied at the Met and the School of American Ballet and danced with the Joffrey, Harkness, and Dance Theatre of Harlem companies and with Jerome Robbins's Ballets: USA; and Billy Wilson, who studied with Karel Shook, danced with the Joffrey, Dutch National, and Netherlands Ballet companies, and became a choreographer and director.

Although not particularly well-known as a choreographer, Corvino, who had started to create student showcases in Uruguay, choreographed and directed a full-length *Nutcracker* at SUNY-Purchase in 1989 and 1990. He had previously presented his version of the popular seasonal classic ballet with the New Jersey Dance Theatre Guild in the 1970s. Eleanor D'Antuono, then a principal dancer with American Ballet Theatre, danced the lead in 1974 in what the *Woodbridge News Tribune* called "a traditional Petipa-Ivanov version recreated by Alfred Corvino." Other well-known ballerinas who danced the leading Sugar

Plum Fairy role for these performances included Maria Scalia (1969), Christine Sarry (1970–73 and 1975), and Joyce Cuoco (1976–77).

The New Jersey Dance Theatre Guild was created by a group of New Jersey ballet teachers who wanted help training their young students and also wanted to improve their own technique. For ten years, Corvino helped them achieve their goal. He served as director of the guild and brought his daughter Andra to serve as ballet mistress for its company. With the opportunity to perform in his version of the *Nutcracker* serving as a catalyst, the young students improved rapidly under Corvino's tutelage.

For the New Jersey Theatre Guild and the Princeton Ballet, Corvino also set a version of Jules Perrot's 1845 ballet *Pas de Quatre* for four leading ballerinas of the era: Fanny Cerito, Lucile Grahn, Carlotta Grisi, and Marie Taglioni. Corvino's version was based on his familiarity with Anton Dolin's 1941 version of this famous Romantic-era work. Corvino also choreographed for the Maryland Ballet and for numerous productions of the Amato Opera, a New York City–based chamber opera group. In 1976, he danced the roles of Herr Drosselmeyer in the New Jersey Dance Theatre Guild's production of the *Nutcracker* and Dr. Coppelius in a production of *Coppélia* by the Classical Ballet Company of New Jersey.

Corvino's most unusual choreography was seen on the stage of the Roxy Theatre in New York in the week beginning January 21, 1953. Here, on what was called the "Ice Colorama," a stage revue on ice entitled *Rollicking Rhythm* was presented. Although Tony Charmoli was the resident choreographer at the Roxy, there were two duets presented that week, *Deep Purple* and *The Blue Danube*, both with "ballet choreography" by Alfredo Corvino. He found no difficulty shifting from ballet slippers to ice skates and recalled the endeavor as "great fun." His biography in the program mentioned that he had been a boxer and also stated that he had been the resident choreographer for the Montevideo Municipal Ballet. Corvino never mentioned the latter. It is possible that this credit related to some of the student performances that he directed with Pouyanne. Corvino had no further records pertaining to this, nor have any been found, and he died before the issue could be pursued.

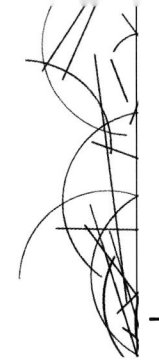

Chapter 6

FROM BROOKLYN TO MANHATTAN: THE EXTENDED CORVINO FAMILY

When Marcella Rubin returned from Ohio to her parents' home and business as a mature, attractive, confident woman and as part owner of the family house, she would sometimes invite people to dinner, most of them new friends and acquaintances from the Russian Tea Room set. She and her mother took turns with the cooking chores, a ritual they always followed. Corvino attended Marcella's dinner parties at least once before the army and many times after his return to New York.

After Marcella and Alfredo married and settled into the renovated one-room basement apartment of the Rubins' house at 1860 East 7th Street in Brooklyn, both families often had dinner together. At this point, Alfredo assumed responsibility for the Rubins' mortgage payments, a practice he continued throughout the lives of his in-laws until the mortgage was paid off.

Following the birth of Marcella and Alfredo's daughter Andra, the tenants living on the second floor willingly moved out, saying they could not stand in the way of a young family. The three Corvinos moved upstairs, but most meals were still taken on the first floor with the Rubins. Thus, the Rubin family became the Rubin/Corvino family, and then simply the Corvino family. To this was added the ever-widening circle that was and still is their extended family.

Corvino earned a good living by working nonstop. He supported everyone. Isabel helped out by taking care of the girls. Joseph, a gentle figure, would bring his granddaughters candy when he returned home from his job in the city, sitting them on his lap while singing songs and reciting poems.

Religiously, it was an ecumenical household. Isabel said that Alfredo looked more Jewish than any of their relatives, and Marcella always felt he was more Jewish than she in terms of his unswerving ethical values. Neither Marcella nor Alfredo (born Catholic) subscribed to an organized religion. Instead, they celebrated any and every holiday, always with lively company. In December, there was a Christmas tree at one end of the living room and a Chanukah menorah at the other. Ernesta remembers asking her grandmother what religion they believed in. Her answer was "we believe in kindness." Neither Alfredo nor Marcella were particularly physically demonstrative, although her verbal warmth and actions and his quiet but steady presence assured their daughters they were loved. The extended family all felt the same way.

Marcella described the physical setting of the first floor of the family house as a large, pleasant area in which the kitchen opened up into the dining room, making them almost one room. There was also a separate living room and a closed-in porch. The round dining table had an extension, and when opened, it seated twelve people easily. Guests included Isabel's family, Joseph's family, Alfredo's friends, Marcella's friends, and assorted ballet people. Sometimes they came during the week, other times on weekends, and always on holidays. A New Year's Eve party was an established tradition, with friends and Joseph's family attending. It is an annual event that Ernesta still keeps, and dancers from many different generations and places come to stay for an hour or for the entire evening.

A Home, a Salon, a Symposium

After their marriage and the establishment of Brooklyn as the Corvinos' home, a whole new group of people began visiting on Sundays and holidays—what Marcella referred to as "the Cunningham crowd," meaning dancers from the Merce Cunningham Dance Company and school. Cunningham, a principal dancer with the Martha Graham Dance Company, began presenting his own works in 1942. Unlike Graham's choreography, which often expresses the struggles of archetypal female heroines, Cunningham's choreography is concerned with time and space and the possible relationships between the two. His own background included ballet training, and his dancers were well versed in ballet technique. Cunningham technique, as taught at his studio, contains elements of both Graham and ballet.

In Corvino, this group of dancers found a teacher who could explain movement as a pure entity in the same way that Cunningham used it choreographically. Although they all studied with Margaret Craske, who some found impersonal, and some studied with Antony Tudor, Corvino was a more accessible and engaging teacher, eager and willing to participate in lengthy discussions and to answer their innumerable questions. They wanted to get additional information from Corvino about such things as placement and musicality. Marcella said they were able to ask questions and have them answered on the spot. Reflecting on these occasions, she felt that the insightful, almost Socratic discussions were "a very precious way" to keep these dancers dancing longer. With her natural affinity for clear explanations and her understanding of her husband's approach, Marcella probably contributed to Corvino's informal tutorials.

The "Cunningham crowd" included Remy Charlip, Bruce King, Viola Farber, and Carolyn Brown, in addition to dance students from the Met and Juilliard. Brown, a superb dancer, graduated from Wheaton College and attended Juilliard, where she studied with Tudor and Craske and was Cunningham's leading dancer for twenty years. Farber trained with Craske, was a founding member of the Cunningham company, and in 1968, created her own company. She later became director of the dance department at Sarah Lawrence College. King, from California, danced in many other modern dance companies, formed his own in 1970, and also taught. Charlip was an artist, playwright, and choreographer; the cofounder of the Paper Bag Players (a children's theater); and a member of the Judson Dance Theater.

The large, inclusive, encompassing family concept was important to both Marcella and Alfredo. Marcella and her mother enjoyed entertaining and holding court. Alfredo enjoyed having people around and talking about dance. In his quiet way, he welcomed everyone. Hard of hearing ever since a bout with diphtheria in early childhood, Corvino seemed at times somewhat remote or disengaged. It took a lot of concentration for him to sort out conversations in the din of the large, vivacious crowd that gathered in Marcella's bountiful open kitchen. Later in life, he sought help through a hearing aid and always regretted not having done so sooner.

Happily for Corvino, Marcella was there to hear the tales about all aspects of the dancers' lives and to comment thoughtfully. She was not only a good listener but also had the ability to observe visually. She possessed an amazing insight into people, whom she could size up immediately, a quality Alfredo recognized and honored. What was also constant in the family was a creative energy that was present in the immediate family interactions and that was expanded and enhanced by the ever-varying influx of visitors.

Alfredo traveled constantly in the early years of their marriage, and for weeks at a time in the last decade of his life. Marcella preferred to stay at home and at the school, where she felt entirely comfortable and fulfilled in her role. She never had any desire to travel with Alfredo and never visited Uruguay. Later in life, she suffered from agoraphobia and emphysema and endured bouts of depression. When they were at home alone, Alfredo enjoyed carpentry projects and fixing things around the house. He also relished working on the engine of his car, possibly remembering the days when Montevideo was known as a center for antique automobiles.

No one in the family hesitated to invite guests home for a meal, an overnight stay, or a longer sojourn. These guests and extended "family members" moved away, raised families, opened schools, and started dance companies but, somehow or other, always kept in touch. They would drop in unannounced at the oddest times and telephone or e-mail from all over the world.

A Brownstone in Manhattan

The Corvinos' decision to move to Manhattan was made because Alfredo was driving there, and numerous other places, seven days a week. The new house, a brownstone at 451 West 50th Street, between Ninth and Tenth avenues, was purchased in June 1961. Alfredo said he contributed three-quarters of the payment. However, the deed was in Isabel's and Marcella's names, one-third and two-thirds, respectively. Who made the decision regarding the deed and the reasons behind it are unknown. Andra and Ernesta say their father was curious as to why his name was never put on anything, but since he trusted their mother completely and let her handle all money matters, including investments, he said little.

The closing took place on February 21, 1961. Marcella and Isabel are listed as "purchasers" and Alfredo as "husband." He signed the initial check for $5,000, however, and the mortgage on this $24,000 purchase was paid in full—by Alfredo—by January 1964. When Isabel died in 1968, her share of the house was left to Phil and Carryl, and Alfredo purchased their shares after much haggling and histrionics on their part. The deed was then changed to read "Marcella and Alfredo Corvino."

The ground floor of the brownstone, with its own entrance and garden in the rear, was originally the 451 Club, a men's club for what Marcella called "the Irish guys" in the neighborhood. Larry, a big, heavy man, was the president and ruled over the club's pool table, bar, radio, television, and several easy chairs. The top floor also had tenants, so the new Corvino/Rubin family settled into the two middle floors, but only after extensive renovations to repair the damage they found from cascades of water that had poured into this area of the house (either unbeknownst to the members of the men's club below or of no great interest to them). The Rubins lived on the third floor, and Marcella, Alfredo, Andra, and Ernesta created a home on the second floor, where the girls shared a large bedroom. All meals, however, were eaten together on the third floor.

The house next door was a brothel run by "Mademoiselle Isabella." Very often the Corvinos' doorbell would ring, and a man would ask for Isabelle. The girls—and sometimes Alfredo—would politely ask him to be seated and would get Isabel Rubin, who would come downstairs, point, and shout, "Next door!" Much hilarity ensued, as Alfredo and his daughters enjoyed this ongoing, oft-repeated comedy of errors, their laughter forging a fun-loving bond among them.

Just one year after the purchase of the brownstone, in 1962, Joseph Rubin died and the 451 Club moved to a new location. Both developments created many changes in the Corvino family's new home. The Corvinos took over the ground floor and began a major renovation. Most of this was done by outside workers, with Marcella checking everything upon her return from work, since Alfredo was gone day and night teaching. Isabel undoubtedly also kept a piercing eye on the workers' daily progress. Andra remembers rehearsing for a performance in the gutted area, an indication of how the family integrated each and every event in their lives, turning it to creative ends if possible. When this ground floor renovation was complete, the Corvinos had a new living room, a large kitchen, a dining room (in which the well-used round dining table was the central focus), a bedroom in the rear, and access to the much-coveted garden. Isabel moved down into the new bedroom, and they all gathered in the expansive family rooms for meals and socializing.

The third-floor apartment was rented out to what Andra refers to as "a series of horrors," until, finally, Edilio Ferraro, one of Alfredo's students, moved in. He danced with the Metropolitan Opera Ballet and later became involved in Pilates and massage therapy. Helpful and close to the family, he was, according to Andra, "like a big brother."

In 1968, when Isabel died, Andra moved into her grandmother's bedroom on the ground floor, leaving Ernesta the large room on the second floor to herself. All this time, the extended family gatherings continued around the always over-laden dining table, spilling into the garden in warm weather.

Andra

Andra Corvino was born April 6, 1948, at Madison Park Hospital in Brooklyn. She jokes that she was a honeymoon baby and, given the moral conservatism of that era, is glad that she was not born any earlier. She remembers being a happy child, always surrounded by different people. She was outgoing and sociable, talked early, and danced freely whenever and wherever she could. She was taken to rehearsals at an early age and watched them sitting on her mother's lap. She was not yet four when her father taught her how to balance by having *passé*-holding contests with her. She feels her attraction to dance was partly genetic and partly due to the fact that she saw so much of it, all around her.

Andra went to P.S. 23 in Brooklyn and was scheduled to attend her mother's alma mater, Abraham Lincoln High School, a plan that changed when the family moved to Manhattan. The move to this culture-rich borough caused Andra to think about the possibility of herself becoming part of a theatrical environment. In consultation with her mother, she decided to go to a professional school. Andra considered attending the High School of Performing Arts, but in 1961, the school did not have enough applicants to create a freshman class in the Drama Department, where she wished to study. Instead, she attended Professional Children's School for a year but did not like it. After a year, she transferred to Quintano's School for Young Professionals. Located in the Eileen O'Connor Dance Studios on West 56th Street, the school offered small classes to students who were also working models or actors.

Andra was very single-minded and determined in her goal to be in the theater. In addition to the dance classes she began to take at the Metropolitan Opera Ballet School, she also studied voice, enjoyed acting, and loved musical theater and opera. She had an agent while still in elementary school. There was an older girl studying at the Met, and her mother, Mrs. Leichman, took Andra to audition for a summer theater production of *Cat on a Hot Tin Roof* at the Long Beach Playhouse on Long Island. She played the part of one of Big Daddy and Big Momma's grandchildren and lived with the Leichmans for the summer. They introduced her to Mildred Green, an agent who sent her to audition for various musicals. Among the jobs she obtained was a part in the Theater Guild's television production of *One Red Rose for Christmas*, starring Helen Hayes and Patty Duke.

Andra's formal dance training began at the Met. She was eight years old and attended class once a week with Miss Curtis, born and trained in Britain. Instead of dancing, however, Andra took refuge under the piano. Finally, Curtis talked to Marcella about her daughter's lack of participation. When Marcella asked her daughter if there was a reason for this, Andra replied that she had been under the impression that she, Andra, would teach the class. Marcella decided she was not yet ready to study ballet.

By the next year, however, Andra was ready to enroll once again, and Margaret Craske, the director of the school, assigned her to study with Mattlyn Gavers, whose class for slightly older children Andra had previously observed. Gavers, also occasionally known by her family name of Gevurtz-Gavers, was from Utah, where she later taught at the University of Utah and worked with Willam Christensen at Ballet West. She also staged works for many opera companies, including at the Met during the 1958–59 season. Gavers thought Andra "didn't show off enough."

Andra was ten when, at her father's suggestion, she started studying twice a week with Craske, who she thought was "ancient." Nevertheless, Craske related well to children and had a wonderful sense of humor. The next year, Andra repeated the class as Craske's demonstrator.

Andra feels she learned how to teach from Craske, who eventually let her assist in the children's classes by taking care of the slower students in the back. She says Craske had real knowledge about the human body, and her Cecchetti point of view was body-centered and musical. Craske's children's curriculum was based on her own experiences with Cecchetti, yoga, and folk dance.

When she was fourteen, Andra began to take Antony Tudor's professional/advanced class in the morning. At about the same time, she started to take weekly classes with her father, in *pas de deux*, or partnering. He felt she was old enough and had a solid enough technical background to deal with the father-daughter learning relationship.

By this time, Andra was performing constantly. Gavers was the ballet mistress at the Met in the late 1950s and early 1960s and hired Andra as an extra dancer for many productions. Gavers was also the choreographer for the Little Orchestra Society, which produced ballets danced for and by children. For three seasons, Andra performed with them at the Hunter College Playhouse in *Celeste* and *The Happy Prince*. She also supered in the Met opera productions, playing the

Prince in *Lohengrin* (Wagner) and one of the handmaidens in *Adriana Lecouvreur* (Cilea), among many other roles.

When she was eighteen, Andra found a job as a gofer at the National Music League, an arts management organization. She had graduated from high school, and there was not enough paid dance work to keep her busy. A man named Buddy Rosten, who was the husband of a student of Craske's, told Craske that the league needed a paid intern. Craske passed the information along to Marcella, and from September to December 1966, Andra spent the workweek copying Japanese names and addresses from the telephone book so that they could be mailed flyers announcing the Carnegie Hall premiere of a young Japanese violinist.

On weekends, Andra rehearsed as a principal dancer with the Baltimore City Ballet, directed by Danny Diamond. She performed in, among others, *Brahms' Waltzes*, choreographed by Diamond, and Dolin's *Pas de Quatre* and *La Ventana* (Lumbye and Holm), choreographed by Bournonville. The latter was taught by someone in Baltimore who had seen and learned it but was not authorized to restage it.

Beginning with Andra's first professional work with the Met, for which she was paid by the performance, Marcella deposited all her daughter's earnings into a bank account that was for Andra's use only. In retrospect, Andra felt this served the dual purpose of acknowledging her ability to manage her own life and teaching her how to handle her finances.

Just after Andra turned nineteen, the Met held an audition for dancers. Andra, who had been covering for others but was not a full member of the company, was now formally accepted into the fold. She was not only offered a contract, but Kathleen Crofton, a teacher at the school, implied that she was grooming her for bigger things. In addition to dancing in the operas at the Met, Andra participated in the occasional Ballet Evening, dancing in Fokine's *Les Sylphides*, Dolin's *Pas de Quatre*, and two of Tudor's works, *Echoing of Trumpets* (Martinu) and *Concerning Oracles*, a premiere to music by Ibert. She termed the latter one of his "misses."

The Royal Ballet of England came to the Met every four years, and Andra started dancing as an extra with them when she was ten. She was in her early twenties when the Royal Ballet brought Kenneth MacMillan's *Romeo and Juliet* (Prokofiev), with Anthony Dowell and Rudolf Nureyev alternating in the role of Romeo. When Nureyev was performing as Romeo, Andra appeared as the bride in Romeo's dream in act II, scene I. In the dream, Romeo performs a dance to the mandolin and then kisses the bride. Several company members warned Andra that Nureyev might try to knock her down as they descended the tall, shallow staircase of the set together, which he did attempt to do. She grabbed his hand, forcefully preventing this, and he was so furious that he kissed her smack on the lips rather than on the cheek, as she was expecting.

There had never been any discussion at home with either her father or her mother about what path Andra's career should take. She made decisions on her own and, as in the earlier case of choosing a high school, then consulted her mother. Yet, somehow, everyone concerned knew that she would continue to pursue her career in dance after high school. Marcella always stressed how independent and definite Andra was, calling her willful and stubborn. Marcella could be compassionate and indicate her love for her daughter, but there was much "head butting" between the two.

Andra did not feel comfortable asking her father for guidance, but when she started studying regularly with him at age twenty, he was supportive and would occasionally say things like, "You're a natural on *pointe*." She was a professional dancer now, and he was her mentor. They began to communicate on an almost nonverbal level. He was also more physically demonstrative than her mother, and Andra always felt she had his unconditional support.

By this time, Andra had been at the Met almost two years, and between dancing onstage and in workshops, taking classes, and teaching, she became seriously overworked. From September to June, she rarely saw sunlight. Her father often asked her, "Why are you accepting this job?" but didn't elaborate. She became ill and was hospitalized when she was twenty-one. Her glands were awry, and she was released from the hospital after being put on hormone therapy. Andra returned to the Met in 1970 for a while but left again in 1972 after Alicia Markova, whom the dancers loved and respected, was replaced as director of the ballet by Milko Sparemblek.

Meanwhile, in December 1968, at Marcella's urging, Alfredo finally began to fulfill his lifelong dream of opening his own studio. Dance Circle, as the studio was called, was a true family business, with all the Corvinos pitching in and playing their part. Marcella was the school administrator, and Alfredo the director. Andra and Ernesta completed the faculty.

Participating in the renovations of the studio on Eighth Avenue and teaching on the faculty helped to refocus Andra's energies. While teaching at Dance Circle, she continued her performing career, working with the Ruby Shang Dance Company, the Roberto Cartagena Dance Company, and the Opera Company of New York.

Andra had actually begun her teaching career much earlier—and quite unexpectedly—when she was fourteen years old. At that time, she was studying with Antony Tudor at the Met Ballet school. Marcella was working as the school administrator and was in the studio one day, taking attendance, when Tudor lost his temper with the class and told Marcella to find someone who could fill in for him immediately, adding, "Get Andra." Andra was sitting in the dressing room when her mother came rushing in and told her to go teach Tudor's beginning/intermediate class.

Andra's first professional teaching job was at Ramblerny, an estate in Pennsylvania that had been turned into a theater arts camp. In 1965 and 1966, Alfredo was engaged to teach the advanced class, and Andra was hired to teach the beginning and intermediate levels. She then went on to teach at the New Jersey Dance Theatre Guild and Montclair State College, where she covered both ballet and dance history. Her transition from performer to teacher was a gradual one, since in many respects she had always taught, whether covering for Tudor or assisting Craske. She never made a formal break from dancing, and up until 1997, she was still performing baroque dance.

After her father retired from Juilliard, Benjamin Harkarvy, then director of the Dance Division, hired Andra to fill in for a faculty member who was on leave. Harkarvy was a highly respected teacher and choreographer who believed in training dancers free of any mannerisms. He had been artistic director of the Royal Winnipeg Ballet, the Netherlands Dance Theatre, the Harkness Ballet, the Dutch National Ballet, and the Pennsylvania Ballet. He headed the dance division at Juilliard from 1992 until his death in 2002. Much to Andra's surprise and delight, Harkarvy invited her to return the next year as a full-time member of the ballet faculty, a position she currently holds. She also spent several years as the supervisor of the summer dance program at Juilliard.

Ernesta

When Ernesta Corvino was born on February 27, 1952, in the same hospital as her sister, Andra was very excited about being allowed to help take care of her baby sister. This second daughter, whom Marcella always called "baby," was silent and introverted. She could talk, but only did so to her mother and Andra. Isabel called her "schuma," which is Yiddish for mute. She clung to her mother's skirts, was extremely shy with strangers, and thought that people smiling were laughing at her. Ernesta's memory of her childhood, reinforced by old family films, begins with her sister, Andra, a very feminine, outgoing individual who was always dancing. Ernesta, who liked to observe rather than perform, thought this was silly and much preferred playing alone in the house, garden, or garage in Brooklyn. When she was five, she would take the subway to the city with Andra and, in her words, "hang out" with Marcella at the Met.

Her mother took her to political rallies and started to teach her reading and math before she began formal schooling. Ernesta displayed the Corvino ingenuity when she used the television dials to practice her addition and subtraction. She attended kindergarten at P.S. 238 but, painfully shy, hated it. At age five, surgery to remove a cyst behind her right ear required a six-day stay at New York University Hospital, which she recalls as "a dungeon." An observant social worker there changed Ernesta's life when she insightfully suggested that her shyness could also be a form of hostility. Recognizing the truth of this observation eventually led her to a conscious effort to develop her social side.

Ernesta was nine when the family moved from Brooklyn to Manhattan, where she began attending P.S. 111 at 52nd Street and Tenth Avenue. Encouraged by a teacher there, she began to emerge as a potential leader. She also started to make friends. By the time she reached Jr. H.S. 17, a fairly tough school, she had learned not to be afraid of people who were different and, equally fearlessly, to be herself. She followed Andra to Quintano's, where she happily made friends she still sees. She graduated in 1970 as a straight A student. In 1972, she received an AA degree in liberal arts from the Borough of Manhattan Community College and completed a BA in English, graduating with honors from the State University of New York Empire State College in Manhattan in 2006.

Ernesta says she fell in love with the theater after she began kindergarten. She enjoyed entering into a place of make-believe with singers, dancers, and other artists whose expressiveness encouraged her to emerge from her interior and insular hiding place. She started pre-ballet at the Met with Karen Kanner when she was six and disliked it, saying it was not real ballet and was boring. Her parents said the lessons would always be there if she wanted them but didn't insist that she take them. She grudgingly continued of her own accord. By her second year, she was studying with Craske and Bunty Kelly. By the time Ernesta reached her teens, her teachers included Tudor, Kathleen Crofton, Yurek Lazowski, and her father. She also took modern classes with José Limón and Joyce Trisler. She thinks there was always a part of her that wanted to be a dancer but would not admit it because she wanted to assert her individuality within the family.

Ernesta became a horse lover when she was eleven. An older student at the Met talked constantly about horses and gave her a gift of jodhpurs and a riding shirt for her eleventh birthday. Her father took her for riding lessons in New Jersey on Sundays. When she switched to the Claremont Academy on West 89th Street in Manhattan, Alfredo took riding lessons himself and even entered a horse show. This provided a new sort of father-daughter bond, as did her interest in cars.

When she was very young, they walked together on Coney Island Avenue in Brooklyn, and she learned from him the make and model of every car they passed along the way.

Ernesta says her father did not understand her lack of conformity or her eccentricities, which perplexed, worried, and sometimes amused him. He was afraid she would take her nonconformity too far someday, and they often clashed. When, as an adult, she was ready to discuss the fact that she was gay, she first told her mother, then Andra, and a few months later, her father. She felt that after this conversation, he began to see her differently and to better understand who she was. She feels they taught each other a great deal, if at times warily.

Ernesta and Marcella, however, shared everything and talked incessantly. To Ernesta, her mother was "Mother Bear"—protective, smart, wise, and sharing. Marcella was her champion, and their respect and affection were mutual.

Ernesta started performing children's roles when she was seven, first with the Metropolitan Opera, then with visiting ballet companies and the New York Shakespeare Festival. She was nine when the Kirov Ballet came from what was then Leningrad (now St. Petersburg), and as a result of Craske's recommendation, she danced "Hop O' My Thumb" in Petipa's *Sleeping Beauty* (Tchaikovsky). When, in the summer of 1964, the New York Shakespeare Festival presented *A Midsummer Night's Dream*, Ernesta was the fairy Moss, under the direction of Jack Sydow. She also went out in the festival's mobile theater to different parks around the city, which she found frightening at times, due to the prevailing climate of simmering racial unrest in many neighborhoods throughout the five boroughs.

At age fourteen, Ernesta was a soloist with the Baltimore City Ballet, and by that time, she had appeared with other small ballet and modern companies, including those of Ruby Shang, Seamus Murphy, and the American Chamber Ballet. In 1970–71, she performed with the Metropolitan Opera Ballet, and from 1972 to 1974 she was a member of the Radio City Music Hall Ballet. Seeking opportunities to develop her versatility as a dancer, Ernesta also spent five seasons with the New York Baroque Dance Company and appeared in *From the Horse's Mouth*, a form of dance/documentary created by Tina Croll and James Cunningham. From 1968 to 1979, she danced with her father's Dance Circle company—a performing group associated with the family's Dance Circle studio. In 1981, she established Ernesta Corvino's Dance Circle Company to explore her own choreographic vision. The company performed in many venues and was presented for several seasons by the Riverside Dance Festival on Manhattan's Upper West Side.

Ernesta's teaching experience began at Dance Circle when she was sixteen and still a student. Here, over a twenty-five-year period, she taught all aspects of ballet technique, including character, *pas de deux*, *pointe*, men's class, and special classes in the technique of turning. She also taught classes in baroque dance and hatha yoga. In addition, she spent four years teaching at the Inner City Ensemble in Paterson, New Jersey, and five years at the Governor's School of New Jersey. Ernesta has taught ballet for several different companies, including the José Limón company. She has been an instructor at Sarah Lawrence College, SUNY-Purchase, Randolph-Macon College, Long Island University–Brooklyn, and Hofstra University. Since 1995, she has been an artist-in-residence at the University of Nevada at Las Vegas for one semester each year.

Since her first choreographic collaboration with her father, on *The Nutcracker* for the New Jersey Dance Theatre Guild in 1969, Ernesta has always been interested in choreography. She has created works for colleges, dance groups, and soloists, as well as the Dance Circle company and her own company. She currently teaches privately and for the José Limón Dance Company and has taken her father's place as ballet mistress with Tanztheater Wuppertal Pina Bausch.

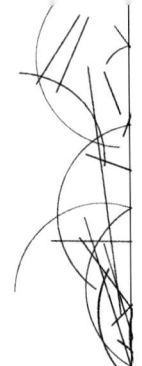
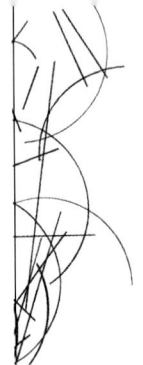

Chapter 7

Major Teaching Venues

Corvino's three major teaching venues—the places where he taught and influenced the greatest number of students—were the Metropolitan Opera Ballet School, the Juilliard School, and Dance Circle.

The Metropolitan Opera School

In the late 1940s, Corvino was dancing at the Met, taking classes with Tudor and Craske, and teaching at different studios in and around Manhattan. In 1951, Tudor relinquished his post as artistic director of the Metropolitan Opera Ballet company and became head of the new ballet program at Juilliard. Corvino started teaching an evening class at the Met, in addition to substituting for Mattlyn Gavers and Kate Forbes, who taught the children's classes. By this time, seeing how lucrative the ballet school had become, the Metropolitan Opera decided to incorporate it once again under its administrative aegis. Craske and Tudor remained in their positions as faculty member and director, respectively.

By September 1953, Corvino had a contract with the Met Ballet School stating that for the school year from September 8 through June 19, he would teach five regular one-and-a-half-hour classes, plus one intermediate class every other week. For this he was to be paid $60 per week, plus $12.50 for each additional class taught. This Met contract, and all subsequent ones, stated that he was an instructor under Antony Tudor and that he had to join the relevant labor organizations at his own expense. As the years went on, the number of Corvino's teaching hours increased, as did his salary, with the contracts eventually covering thirty-nine or forty weeks of the year. By the 1956–57 academic year, Corvino was teaching eleven hours a week and substituting for Gavers when she was on tour. In 1958–59, he taught nine one-and-a-half-hour classes and two one-hour classes for a salary of $146 per week. By 1960, he was receiving a weekly salary of $160.

Corvino stopped teaching at the Met School when it closed in 1968, by which time he and Craske were being given equal billing as faculty. After being associated with the Met for more than twenty years—as both a dancer and teacher—Corvino received a thank-you letter and a check for $400 when he was terminated at the Metropolitan Opera Ballet School, a paltry and graceless gesture that, even years later, astounded him.

The ostensible reason for the school's closing was that it was too expensive to run. Much of the blame was placed on the expensive union contracts of stagehands, which included time-and-a-half pay for overtime. One of the main responsibilities of the stagehands at the school was the setting up of the *barres* in the studios before each class and taking them down again after class when the studios were used for rehearsal. But the Corvinos felt that the real reason for the closing was that the School of American Ballet was scheduled to move into the newly built Lincoln Center, and Lincoln Kirstein could not envision the New York City Ballet, the Metropolitan Opera, and Juilliard all having separate ballet programs.

Kirstein was a brilliant, multitalented, and enigmatic Harvard-educated Bostonian who, in 1933, convinced the young Russian-trained George Balanchine to come to the United States to create an American ballet. Kirstein was the producing force behind what Balanchine deemed the necessary school—the School of American Ballet (SAB)—as well as the three companies that preceded the New York City Ballet. The State Theater at Lincoln Center became the new home of the company in 1964, and when Juilliard moved to Lincoln Center in 1969, the dance division was given just two studios there rather than the six that they had originally been promised, with the other four going to SAB. Kirstein was a powerful, if discreet, protector and advocate for the New York City Ballet and SAB. Though he operated largely behind the scenes, he was highly proprietary and territorial. Any perceived competitive threats to his beloved and carefully nurtured school and company, especially from within Lincoln Center, would be met and countered gracefully but firmly.

Marcella's Role at the Met

There is a memorandum in the Met archives addressed to Herman Krawitz from Marcella Corvino, dated December 12, 1958, in which she suggests some changes to Mr. Corvino's letter of agreement in regard to his teaching hours and salary. Marcella wrote this memo in her capacity as administrative secretary to both the school and the company, but she was also in effect delivering her husband's employment demands.

Just as Alfredo and Andra occasionally found themselves in plum jobs through happenstance, Marcella had gained her post at the Met quite by accident, as an emergency and presumably temporary substitute. One day, in 1957, she received a telephone call from Tudor. Kathleen Harding, the administrative secretary of the ballet school at the Met, had suddenly become ill and had been hospitalized. Could Marcella come and sit in the office for a few hours as her substitute? Harding died soon thereafter, and Marcella filled the job until the school closed in 1968, after which she briefly worked in two other departments of the Metropolitan Opera. As administrative secretary for the ballet school, she had many responsibilities. Among other tasks, she collected money and took attendance, often with Ernesta clinging to her skirts. When Andra was old enough to travel by subway, the two sisters would go to the Met together after school. Later in the evening, when Alfredo and Marcella were both finished working at the school, they would all pile into the car, and the girls would fall asleep on the drive back to Brooklyn.

Marcella's memories of those years centered on the students, many of them young. She remembered getting calls from her husband telling her to "sneak" people into class because he felt they were talented but feared an audition with Craske would be too intimidating and would frighten them away. Often the Corvinos paid for these classes when the young dancers-to-be, many of them Juilliard students, could not afford them.

The emotional climate at the school was often fraught. Craske and Tudor had been feuding for many years. Each had his or her own devoted followers among the dancers. Marcella maintained a strictly professional and neutral relationship with both Craske and Tudor. The dancers often came to hang out and talk to her because she had the ability to listen to everyone. She said that being in the center of this maelstrom of love and hate was often difficult, but no one, including her husband, wanted her to leave the job.

Alfredo was entirely unaware of the Craske-Tudor feud, and Marcella didn't tell him anything about it. He worked with both Craske and Tudor, and they were always pleasant to each other in his presence. Occasionally, there would be a faculty meeting of the three, which Marcella also attended in order to take notes. Yet the intra-faculty bickering often rendered note-taking moot. "I didn't have a single note because the arguments would start about what was right."

At their last faculty meeting, Tudor suggested they discuss the mazurka—how you break it down and how you teach it to men. Marcella remembered Corvino saying, "Why start with mazurka? Let's start with basics—very definite positions of the feet, the arms, the directions of the body. It's very simple, although not easy." Tudor picked up his things, put them in his pocket, and never mentioned another meeting. Craske was silent and also left.

Tudor told Craske he was sorry they were locked into the Cecchetti syllabus, but she refused to depart from it. In the spring of 1952, Craske gave a review course for teachers in the Cecchetti method, which Corvino took because he was expected to do so. Yet he found a way to teach through and around the syllabus. Corvino used the Cecchetti method as a framework, but in his classes he also incorporated

Bournonville technique and the French approach that he had learned from Pouyanne and others.

The Juilliard School

Around 1950, William Schuman, a composer and the president of the Juilliard School, one of the outstanding music conservatories in the world, invited Martha Hill, a well-known dance educator from Ohio, to design and run a dance program.

Hill (1900–1995), trained in ballet, modern dance, and Dalcroze Eurhythmics, with degrees from Teachers College, Columbia University, and New York University (NYU), had been a member of the Martha Graham company from 1929 to 1931. She taught at many universities, was the director of the Bennington School of the Dance and of the dance program at NYU, and was a founder of the American Dance Festival. Her organizational talent, boundless energy, and ability to connect with almost every participant in American dance made her a unique individual and an excellent choice to head the new Juilliard Dance Division, a position she held until 1983.

The Juilliard Dance Division opened in September 1951, initially offering a BS degree in dance. The BFA degree that replaced it was introduced in 1963. Students majored in either ballet or modern and, if the latter, had to choose between Graham and Limón technique. Hill gathered a faculty of the most illustrious figures in the American dance scene—Martha Graham, Doris Humphrey, José Limón, Antony Tudor, Margaret Craske—to teach in a program that was based on the belief that the training of a complete dancer required both ballet and modern training, plus music, composition, dance history, Labanotation, and studies in the humanities. In inviting Tudor to be in charge of ballet, she gave him a certain amount of freedom to craft his program. Hill was adamant, however, that the Cecchetti syllabus be used and carefully outlined for each level.

Tudor not only brought in Corvino to teach in the spring of 1952—the second semester of the division's existence—but by 1954, he had also convinced him to give up performing altogether and devote himself entirely to a career of teaching. Juilliard was then located on Claremont Avenue and West 122nd Street, and the Met was on West 40th Street. There were some days when Corvino taught as many as six classes between the two schools. From 1953 through 1969, he also taught in the Juilliard Preparatory Division, which offered classes for younger students on Saturdays.

The Juilliard catalogue did not list Corvino until the 1953–54 academic year, when the term "assistant" was used after his name, as it was for Ruth Currier, Ethel Winter, Betty Jones, Lucy Venable, and others. By the 1955 catalogue, this differentiating terminology had disappeared. Over the years, Corvino taught Ballet I, II, III, and IV, two classes a day, four days a week. He occasionally taught private pupils sent to him by Juilliard, usually at the Met studios. Corvino also sometimes taught Ballet Arrangements, a euphemism for choreography.

In the eleventh year of the Dance Division, the ballet faculty had come to include Margaret (Maggie) Black, Henry Danton , and Fiorella Keane. "Miss Hill," as she was affectionately called by her students and even many of her faculty, decided to present a ballet program entitled *Gradus ad Parnassum* (*Steps to Parnassus*), referring to the abode of the muses in ancient Greece. It was really a presentation of the ballet syllabus taught at Juilliard, with the initial announcement in the press stating that it would illustrate the various phases of ballet training in progressive order. Performed on March 8 and 9, 1962, in the Juilliard Concert Hall, the first third of the program was called *Ballet Studies* and consisted of five sections: "Ballet I," choreographed by Tudor to music of Antonio Gardeno; another "Ballet I," also by Tudor, to music of Henry Purcell; "Ballet II" choreographed by Maggie Black to music by Ernest Bloch; "Ballet II and III," by Corvino to Federico Mompou's music; and "Ballet III and IV," which used music by Francis Poulenc and was created by Keane.

Tudor evidently decided who would choreograph and direct each section, based to some degree on the levels they taught, although Hill wrote to Corvino asking him to choose some girls from Ballet I level for Tudor to use: "Mr. Tudor asks if you will choose at least five girls in Ballet I level . . . whom he may meet to start something for production to Purcell." The idea for the work had been Hill's, and as was her way of working, she kept control over everything. June Dunbar, her assistant at the time, felt that Tudor had no choice in the matter since he depended for a living upon his Juilliard salary. Tudor tried to stay clear of the term "choreographer" for this production. The "arrangers," as he called them, were left to choose their own music.

Corvino's selection of Mompou's *Scènes d'Enfants* was made because he had seen Clotilde Sakharov dance a solo to this music in Uruguay, and he had wanted to use it ever since. He said Tudor was familiar with the score, which had no bar lines and was played on a piano. Careful to respect Hill's wishes and follow the proper Cecchetti syllabus at Juilliard, he appropriated for his piece the *attitude penché*, the *temps de flèche*, and the freely sweeping weight shift into a *coupé* position that Corvino called *coupé dip*. After viewing it on film many years later, he said that he would change nothing in his choreography and that the dancers were unified and used their torsos well. Ruth Mesavage, a sophomore at the time and one of the four girls in the piece, recalled loving it because the steps were so classical and Corvino so exact in teaching it. She labeled it "a bijou."

In January 1962, William Schuman was appointed president of the newly created and still-being-developed Lincoln Center. He was replaced at Juilliard by another composer, Peter Mennin. As the result of endless meetings between the Juilliard dance faculty, the Juilliard administration, and Lincoln Center officials, the Dance Theater was set to become the premiere dance venue in the new Lincoln Center complex. By the time Juilliard moved to Lincoln Center in 1969, however, the Dance Theater had morphed into the New York State Theater, with the New York City Ballet as its resident company. Four out of the six studios originally envisioned for Juilliard's Dance Division were instead allocated to Kirstein's "baby," the School of American Ballet.

As a result, there was real doubt regarding the survival of the Dance Division. Juilliard archives reveal that Mennin wished to eliminate it. He sent out notices to prospective students saying that, unless adequate funds were obtained, 1970–71 might be the last year of dance training at Juilliard. This prompted a huge outcry and organized resistance by currently enrolled students, led by the fearless and determined Hill, who eventually prevailed. In January 1971, however, it was decided to terminate the ballet major and concentrate on modern dance with ballet studies in a supporting role. Tudor left that same year. By the 1990s, both ballet and modern were again emphasized equally.

All throughout this turbulent time, Corvino kept teaching his classes, ignoring the often volatile politics going on around him. He retired from Juilliard in May 1994 and prepared to proceed to the next phase of his life. In the note he sent to Benjamin Harkarvy, the director of the Dance Division at that time, dated May 17, 1994, he thanked all of the faculty and administration for their presence at the farewell concert ("I was very moved") and for "the years of friendship and support, the shared laughter and woes, and all the experiences that a community such as ours provides."

Juilliard awarded Corvino an honorary doctor of fine arts in 2003. Two years later, he received the Martha Hill Award, established in memory of the indomitable founding dance director and given to an individual for outstanding contribution to dance. Corvino was the first recipient of the award, and the room in which the award dinner was held was packed with dance dignitaries and former students.

Dance Circle

Corvino said he had always wanted a studio of his own—for years he was like a vagabond going from place to place—but when the Met closed, it was Marcella who decided it was time for him and the girls to open a school.

In the 1960s, Corvino taught open classes in New York in a space rented from Jerry LeRoy, on Eighth Avenue between 46th and 47th streets. The studio was right next door to a billiard parlor that was above a stationery store. Marcella said, "Every time we passed the parlor, I would say a little prayer that they would clear out, and one day they were raided because they were selling cocaine. The guy went to jail, and the place was empty."

The entire Corvino family was involved in the twenty-five-year venture that began in 1968 and was called Dance Circle. The name was chosen because Corvino did not want the studio name to include his name, and they all liked the symbolism of a circle. At first, there was a great deal of work to be done: the twelve billiard tables were cleared out, a contractor was hired to put up partitions and make two dressing rooms, and an extra bathroom was added. They did much of the work themselves, helped by students from the Met and Juilliard, who stripped the old linoleum off the floor and painted the walls and ceiling. When the front studio and the slightly larger back studio were finally completed, the Corvinos took out a big advertisement in *Dance Magazine*, but after that, word of mouth was the only advertising needed.

Alfredo was the director of the school, Andra was a faculty member, and Ernesta began her teaching career. Marcella handled the business side, collecting money, taking attendance, obtaining licenses and insurance, and paying bills. Alfredo described her function as "communication" because she knew everyone's first and last name and he could never remember a last name. If she was not there, he would simply post a sign-up sheet.

They started with classes for both children and adults. Corvino taught intermediate and advanced levels, Andra children and *pointe*, and Toni Lacativa, a former student, beginners. Ernesta was the substitute teacher. After three years, they began concentrating on adults, with classes ranging from beginners to professionals. Those taking class were former Met and Juilliard students; current Juilliard students; and dancers from the Cunningham, Taylor, Graham, and Limón companies and every other conceivable company and school, both modern and ballet. In the beginning, the Corvinos rented some studio space to Luigi, the flamboyant jazz teacher, but due to the growing volume of classes, they soon needed it all for themselves.

Dance Circle also featured a performing arm, the Dance Circle Company, directed by Corvino. It was a small pickup group, and its formation actually took place several years prior to the opening of the Dance Circle studio. Under various names, it coincided with Corvino's association with the Federation of Music Clubs and the National Arts Club in New York. For both of these clubs, the company gave performances that included excerpts from classical ballets and duets choreographed by Alfredo and Andra. In addition to Andra and Ernesta, the ensemble included Ali Pourfarrokh, who had been a student at the Met and went on to dance with American Ballet Theatre and the Harkness Ballet; Richard Lyle Thomas, originally a student at the Met and then at Dance Circle; Jan Mickens, a Met and Juilliard student who also danced at the Met; Edilio Ferraro, an advanced pupil who became the Corvinos' tenant; and others.

Earlier, in the late fifties, Corvino had given a series of lectures/ demonstrations in the New York City public schools. Andra thinks that someone from the New York City Board of Education had approached the Met School about this venture, and when neither Tudor nor Craske was interested, Marcella decided that Alfredo could do it. Marcella wrote a basic script that required just six advanced dancers from the Met School (three couples), a small portable *barre*, and a reel-to-reel tape player. The program began with a short *barre* and continued with works ranging from excerpts from Fokine's *Les Sylphides* to *A Russian Princess*, a dance choreographed by Craske to the "Drummer Boy" solo from David Lichine's *Graduation Ball*.

The Met School also gave lectures/demonstrations in places such as nursing homes and senior citizen centers. In the summers of 1962 and 1963, it gave outdoor performances in East Harlem. At this same time, the Met orchestra was also offering artists-in-the-schools projects, and both types of performances were far in advance of similar work done under Title III government grants in the late 1960s.

The Dance Circle Company, or its predecessor, was also a guest at different Dance Congresses organized by Lucille Stoddard, a dance educator who was interested in reaching studio teachers on a national level. The company would perform works such as *Pas de Quatre* (after Dolin) or excerpts from *Giselle*, as Corvino had learned it, and then break them down and discuss them with the teachers at the convention. Stoddard had her own form of notation that was used as the basis for these sessions.

Dance Circle gave Corvino the opportunity to codify some of his ideas about teaching ballet and, since he was in charge, to express them. There is a copy of a neatly typed statement, undoubtedly written in conjunction with Marcella and typed by her, on the purpose and policy of Dance Circle. Dedication to teaching ballet as an art form is the first stated priority. Then there is the recognition that each pupil is an individual and unique, and must therefore be taught with his or her specific needs and aspirations in mind, understanding that every student progresses at a different rate. Dance Circle did not offer degrees or certificates because Corvino regarded this process "as an empty pretension." Finally, the statement of principles talks about "special attention to good physical placement, the understanding of movement, musicality, dynamics, vocabulary, and the tradition of the art." It also mentions the accomplishments of past students and the experience of the faculty, and ends by saying, "The school is small and select so that we can give the best possible instruction to those who choose to study with us."

This statement of purpose and policy is based on Alfredo Corvino's ideas, but it also reveals Marcella Corvino's marketing acumen. Andra once dubbed Dance Circle "the mom-and-pop ballet school in New York City," and in part, that description was the result of the "family feeling" that was created and sustained by Marcella. Garbed in her colorful, tentlike dresses, she made students feel as though they were coming home, and she was always there to listen, talk, and tell amazing stories about people and performances while she was either sewing industriously or smoking nonstop, or both simultaneously. Because this atmosphere was replicated in the Corvino home, many considered the Corvinos to be surrogate family.

Marcella's artistic talents went beyond millinery designs and photography. When she went to work at the Met, she became friendly with the women in the costume department and was able to observe their work and ask questions. When the Royal Ballet came on a visit, a tutu was accidentally left behind. Using it as a model, she began to make tutus for the young students at the school, and word of her talent quickly spread.

Tudor asked Marcella to design and make costumes for Juilliard, and for years students from there and from Dance Circle asked her to create costumes for concerts they were giving as professional dancers. When the New Jersey Dance Theatre Guild produced its numerous

Nutcracker's, she helped with the designs and purchased the fabric. The mothers of the guild would send her the dancers' measurements, and Marcella would send them patterns and a sample costume.

As with other aspects of her life, Marcella was a problem solver in this medium as well. She could make a single costume adapt to different bodies and serve different purposes. When Alfredo danced with Herbert Ross, she made a costume for the ballet *The Thief Who Loved a Ghost*, which she later reworked for *La Loie*, the Loie Fuller solo that was reconstructed and performed by Ellen Kogan, a concert dancer and longtime Dance Circle pupil.

Marcella also did work for television. NBC had a Saturday morning show for children, in color, and hired Ron Sequoia to choreograph an underwater ballet, *The Fisherman and the Mermaid*. Sequoia, a Met Ballet dancer and choreographer from Texas who had studied with Craske, was for a brief time artistic director of the Manhattan Festival Ballet and choreographed for the New York City Opera. He stipulated in his contract that Marcella must do the costumes. She clothed jellyfish, sea horses, a mermaid, fishermen, and coral for the cast of dancers from the Met (in which Andra was the only child performer). Marcella designed and made most of the costumes for the Dance Circle Company and for Ernesta's Dance Circle Company after the former disbanded.

The Dance Circle studio closed its doors in 1993, shortly before its director retired from Juilliard. The rent had tripled, yet the neighborhood had changed for the worse (though the prostitutes plying their trade along Eighth Avenue had actually been around for a while). The Guardian Angels patrol organization moved into the former studio rent-free. Despite Dance Circle's untimely and unheralded demise, however, for a quarter of a century this unique haven made a vast contribution to American dance and its dancers.

A Final Exciting Venture

Alfredo Corvino and Pina Bausch first met in the summer of 1959, when he was invited to teach at the Folkwang School in Essen, Germany.

It was also his first meeting with Kurt Jooss, the head of the school, who told Corvino that he looked like a businessman. The following summer, before Tudor went to teach there, Corvino told him about an exceptional student—Bausch—and Tudor arranged for her to come to Juilliard on a scholarship, where, as a visiting student for the 1960–61 academic year, she studied with both of them.

Bausch was born in Germany in 1940 and studied in Essen with Jooss, Hans Zullig, and Lucas Hoving. In the two years she spent in New York, she danced with the Paul Sanasardo-Donya Feuer Dance Company, the New American Ballet, and the Metropolitan Opera Ballet. She returned to Germany and started performing with Jooss's new company, Folkwang Ballett Essen. Bausch soon began choreographing and, in 1973, was asked to become the artistic director of the Tanztheater Wuppertal, which later changed its name to Tanztheater Wuppertal Pina Bausch. Since 1993, she was artistic director of the Folkwang School. Bausch died unexpectedly of cancer on June 30, 2009

Many consider Bausch the most important post–World War II German choreographer. With other compatriots, she created tanztheater (dance theater), which, in its final form, is really a collage of drama, music, and dance, using the strong emotional elements inherited from pre-war German Expressionism. She also added film, stand-up comedy, text, dance hall music, and variety acts to works that are nonlinear and exhausting, both emotionally and physically. The themes of her early works—loneliness, alienation, and cruelty—were often difficult to watch. Although she was still a keen observer of human behavior, Bausch's later work was more lyrical and even humorous.

In 1993, the Bausch company was performing at the Brooklyn Academy of Music (BAM), and Dominique Mercy, one of the senior company dancers, went to watch Corvino teach class at Juilliard. He was accompanied by Ed Kortlandt, the director of the Dance Academy in Rotterdam, Holland, who was observing the class on the recommendation of a former student. When Kortlandt invited Corvino to Rotterdam, Bausch, on Mercy's suggestion, invited him to come to Wuppertal also. This began a ten-year relationship during which Corvino taught company classes and traveled all over the world—Asia, Europe, South America—spending roughly six months a year with the group. He retired for a year in 2003, when Marcella's health began to fail, but following her death in April 2004, he responded affirmatively to Bausch's invitation to join Tanztheater Wuppertal at the end of June. During the company's spring 2005 New York season at BAM, Corvino taught a daily morning class and then a half-hour warm-up before the night's performance. He was scheduled to rejoin the company in September, but his death in August prevented his much awaited return.

Dominique Mercy says that the first time he watched Corvino teach, he saw vestiges of classes he had taken with Hans Zullig of the Jooss company. He adds that all of Pina Bausch's dancers were happy with this gentle man with the beautiful sense of humor; his presence in the studio emanated healthy waves whose source was a complete philosophy of life. He recalls Corvino saying, "I'm not giving class, I'm teaching."

Corvino said that he and Bausch never talked about dance or his classes. It was a matter of silent mutual agreement. Bausch was always happy to announce his return and sometimes watched the end of his class. Mercy says Corvino's curiosity was incredible; he would attend rehearsals and performances, and then his class combinations would refer to the things he had seen—something Bausch surely observed but did not comment upon.

Corvino knew he was getting frail, and one day he said to Mercy, "I packed. I'm ready." The company was on vacation when they learned of his death on August 2, 2005, and Bausch announced it officially when they regrouped. Mercy reported, "We had nothing to say. We just had to be together and think about him."

The Tanztheater Wuppertal company members collected notes, drawings, and photographs of previous tours that Corvino had accompanied them on. Everyone's favorite photograph was one that was taken in San Francisco. In it, a smiling Corvino wears a scarf jauntily thrown around his neck. Seconds before the photo was snapped, he had just donned this scarf—a birthday present the dancers had given him. Corvino truly relished this last adventure in his dance career. He was never astonished or shocked by what he saw onstage—he just wanted to help those dancers dance it.

LATER PHOTOS
(1950–2000)

23. Corvino backstage in Metropolitan Opera production, circa 1950–51

photo by Joseph Nesbitt, courtesy of the Corvino archives

24. Corvino lifting partner June Evans in Metropolitan Opera production, circa 1950–51

photo by Joseph Nesbitt, courtesy of the Corvino archives

25. Corvino backstage on tour with Metropolitan Opera production of *Aida*, circa 1947

photographer unknown, courtesy of the Corvino archives

26. Choreographer's Workshop production of Herbert Ross's *Caprichos*, Jacob's Pillow Dance Festival, Becket, MA, 1950. Corvino is far right.

photo by John Lindquist, © Harvard Theatre Collection

27. Corvino *(far right)* with Kurt Jooss *(far left)* at the Folkwang School in Essen, Germany, 1959. Pina Bausch can be seen in the background, far left, behind Jooss.

photographer unknown, courtesy of the Corvino archives

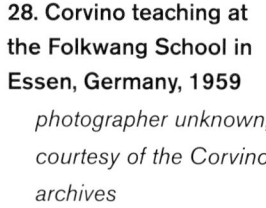

28. Corvino teaching at the Folkwang School in Essen, Germany, 1959

photographer unknown, courtesy of the Corvino archives

29. Metropolitan Ballet School flyer with Corvino, Tudor, and Craske listed as faculty members and Marcella Corvino as secretary, New York City, 1967

courtesy of the Corvino archives

METROPOLITAN OPERA BALLET SCHOOL
1967-1968

Faculty
• TUDOR • CRASKE • CORVINO •

SCHOOL YEAR
September 11th, 1967 through June 22nd, 1968

HOLIDAYS
THANKSGIVING: Thursday, November 23rd, 1967
CHRISTMAS: December 23rd, 1967 through January 1st, 1968 (inclusive)
WASHINGTON'S BIRTHDAY: Thursday, February 22nd, 1968
EASTER: April 12th through April 15th, 1968 (inclusive)
MEMORIAL DAY: Thursday, May 30th, 1968

GENERAL INFORMATION
All fees are payable in advance. No fees are refundable, but in cases of illness, upon presentation of a doctor's certificate, credits for classes missed will be allowed.

Checks to be made payable to: METROPOLITAN OPERA BALLET SCHOOL

Please address all requests for further information to:
MARCELLA CORVINO, Secretary
Metropolitan Opera Ballet School
Lincoln Center Plaza, New York, N. Y. 10023
Telephone: (Area Code 212) 799-3100 Weekdays: 2 to 7:30 P.M.
Saturday: 10 A.M. to 1:30 P.M.

Private academic schooling is available at:
PROFESSIONAL CHILDREN'S SCHOOL
132 West 60th Street, New York, N. Y. 10023
(Within short walking distance of the Metropolitan Opera)

RESIDENCES AVAILABLE FOR GIRLS

THE BARBIZON RESIDENCE Lexington Avenue and 63rd Street	TE 8-5700
THE BRANDON RESIDENCE 340 West 85th Street	SU 7-1212
THE REHEARSAL CLUB 47 West 53rd Street	CO 5-9207
THE LAURA SPELMAN RESIDENCE 840 8th Avenue	CI 6-3700
THE PHOEBE WARREN RESIDENCE 8 East 68th Street	RE 2-1073

30. Corvino confers with Antony Tudor at the piano, circa 1960

photo by Elizabeth Sawyer, courtesy of the Juilliard School archives

31. Corvino teaching at the original Juilliard Dance Division studios at Claremont Avenue and West 122nd St., New York City, 1962

photo by Susan Schiff, courtesy of the Juilliard School archives

32. Corvino teaching at the current Juilliard Dance Division studios in Lincoln Center, New York City, 1976

photo © Peter Schaaf

33. The Dance Circle Company, New York City, 1978 *Pictured from left to right:*
Andra Corvino, Stephen Pier, Ernesta Corvino, Tim Fish, Ellen Field, Colleen
Cavanaugh, Ellen Ashcraft, Joe Fernandez, Joyce Herring, Alfredo Corvino
photo by Les Carr, courtesy of the Corvino archives

34. Fortieth anniversary celebration of the Juilliard Dance Division, New York City,
1992 *Pictured from left to right: Carolyn Adams, Jeanne Ruddy, Jane Kosminsky,*
Clifford Schulman, Martha Hill, Benjamin Harkarvy, Ethyl Winter, Maria Grandy,
Alfredo Corvino, Elizabeth Keen, Laura Glenn, Genia Melikova, Gloria Marina
photo by Stephanie Cimino, courtesy of the Corvino archives

35. Corvino, "the whisper teacher," Paris, 1995

photo © Marion-Valentine, courtesy of the Corvino archives

36. Corvino teaching company class for Tanztheater Wuppertal Pina Bausch, circa 2000

photo © Franceso Carbone

37. Corvino wearing the birthday gift from the Tanztheater Wuppertal dancers, 1999

photo by F. Suels, courtesy of the Corvino archives

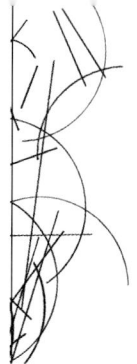

Chapter 8

PHILOSOPHY
AND INFLUENCES

When questioned, Alfredo Corvino often said that he did certain things instinctively. Certainly, much of his philosophy and teaching was the result of his constant experiments with his own body and his unceasing practice, along with his natural sense of line, particularly *épaulement*, alignment, weight, and *ballon* (though he always said that he lacked turn-out).

From the very beginning of his dance life, what Corvino brought to his work was an almost childlike openness—to every idea, every method, and every approach—and after careful consideration, he took from each what he felt he could use. He fervently believed that there was such a thing as basic dance, and that, if taught properly, it would prepare the dancer to perform any style and to perform it longer.

To Corvino, dance was a way of life, and both his living and his teaching were governed by the same philosophy, which emphasized harmony. He avoided studio gossip but could see intimately into his students and their way of working. His warmth and acceptance caused many to relax and love him, yet he never allowed himself to become emotionally entangled in the personal lives of his students.

Corvino felt that the journey toward becoming a dancer was the same as that of becoming a person. Both the body and the person have to fit into the work. He said, "Dancing is dancing, but theatrical dancing is something else. A dancer is made, not born." He believed that in order to learn, the student had to have the ability to reproduce what he or she saw. If a student was not inclined to do this, he felt he could not teach that student. His motto was "Look, think, and then move." This could very easily have come from his early training and participation in sports, particularly boxing, where the shift of weight is of prime importance. In boxing, Corvino had learned that if you look at the opponent's feet, you can tell which way he is going to move. He once said to Beth Hoge, a student, that dance was just like boxing, in that "if you do it wrong, you get hit." He also related the importance of observation and study of movement in dance to driving, where it is necessary to watch the front wheels of the car next to you in order to accurately predict and understand what its intentions and future motions will be and react accordingly with your own effective movements and maneuvers.

Body Mechanics

Corvino had a lifelong fascination with machines, particularly cars, and with the underlying logic and rationality necessary to make something work smoothly, consistently, and reliably. His mother's family all had cars; some even had race cars. His knowledge of motors came from his uncles. He knew how to get the most out of a motor and how to make small modifications to keep it running properly.

When Corvino lived in Brooklyn, he had a garage in which he could work on his car. He bought his first one, a black Studebaker, in 1951, just after he got his driver's license. In 1968, he went to the Robert School on 57th Street, where he took a basic motor course, thinking that in his retirement he would rebuild an old car. He had books on auto mechanics and subscribed to the magazine *Motor Trend*. This was his only hobby.

To Corvino, to train a dancer was to realize that the body is a human machine that is being engineered, crafted, and maintained. Yet, it is a machine with emotions and the ability to think, both of which have an influence on the neuromuscular system. Hence, the teaching of movement was primarily an engineering problem, but secondarily a psychomotor one. Allowing for individual variations, Corvino felt that, in general, the mechanics of movement are the same for everyone—the architecture and joints in the body, the muscles, the nervous system, and the laws of gravity.

To teach is, in part, to build habitual patterns of movement, which can be accomplished only with knowledge of how the body machine works. One day, while teaching, Corvino asked how many students were drivers. He then asked how shock absorbers functioned, related the concept of compression to the knee, and concluded by demonstrating, as illustration, the flexibility of the *plié* to absorb the shock that follows a jump. Corvino also thought a great deal about the concept of hydraulics, which involves the mechanical properties of liquids in motion. He felt his mechanical outlook was originally based on knowledge of the human body, which has its own inherent ways of moving. He would thus use the example of mechanics in trying to share his ideas about the dancer's body with his students.

A Synthesis of Classical and Modern Influences

The Corvino approach to classical ballet technique involves rounded arms, the outward rotation of the limbs, and *aplomb*—all part of the definition of classical ballet (and expounded upon in the later chapter on teaching). Philosophically, Corvino believed in naturalness and simplicity (e.g., the purest possible form of a movement, with no sign of distortion) and acceptance of the fact that each human body is different.

Corvino said that his initial dance influences were European ballet, as he learned it in Montevideo; Spanish dance, as seen throughout Uruguay; and the tango, with its sense of weight, its measured way of moving the entire body in one piece, and its strong relationship to the floor. From Alberto Pouyanne, he learned the basics of ballet, but of more significance to Corvino was the fact that his first teacher taught him to dance every move. Pouyanne passed on what he had learned from Alexandre Volinine, who was renowned for teaching partnering and smooth flowing movements but with an athletic approach. This, plus Pouyanne's training and knowledge as a musician, tapped into his pupil's innate talents.

Corvino's exposure to the Jooss technique and Laban's theories played a major role in his development. A handwritten note in block letters found in his papers reads:

> *I was fortunate to be able to cross the line between ballet and modern dance during a highly creative time. The basic concept of ballet and the Laban technique used in conjunction permit the body its utmost ability to use movement as a means of expression and communication.*

In all probability, this was a quote from Jooss, but the fact that Corvino carefully wrote it out and saved it is significant. Jooss felt there should be no rivalry between different techniques. He was determined to produce a dancer with no mannerisms or discernable style yet knowledgeable about the precise form of ballet and able to move in space as envisioned by Laban. These ideas seem to have coalesced in Corvino's final approach to teaching ballet. They were probably also the reason so many modern dancers felt comfortable studying with him, and why Pina Bausch wanted him as the ballet master for her very expressionist modern dance company.

Corvino said he practiced his own dictum regarding "watching and doing" when he first entered the Jooss company, the style of which included an integration of many of Laban's theories. Laban thought that the inner impulse that originated a movement could be seen as a qualitative use of energy. He also theorized that the natural rhythmic impulses of the body were different from the metric rhythm of music. According to Laban, it was the inner body impulses and emotional attitudes that created the movement qualities he named Flow, Weight, Space, and Time, comparing his theory about movement quality, or dynamics, to the color theory of the painter Wassily Kandinsky.

Laban's concept of weight and the ability to transfer it—creating stability one moment and lability the next in relation to the vertical axis and to gravity—resulted in a wide range of movement patterns in space that Jooss incorporated in his choreography. Corvino felt he picked up the Jooss style easily because he had a good sense of weight. For Laban, Jooss, and Corvino, exploring how to use rhythm and phrasing within a particular spatial pattern imparted a more versatile relationship to that spatial pattern. In addition, exploring the movement qualities in relation to the rhythm and phrasing of the spatial patterns added color to the shape of a movement. In the Jooss company, Corvino really enjoyed these explorations, and he found the results kinesthetically and emotionally satisfying.

Dancing with the Jooss company also gave Corvino extensive exposure to the Dalcroze approach to using the body rhythmically. As described earlier, Elsa Kahl felt Corvino should learn Dalcroze Eurhythmics as a liaison between Laban's ideas and the technique that had become the basis for Jooss's choreography. Although the Dalcroze method begins simply—by relating body movements to musical notes—in its more advanced stages it stresses the ability to create increasingly complex rhythms. Corvino said this made perfect sense to him. He had no difficulty in learning either the Dalcroze or the Laban material because of his training with Pouyanne, which, he later recognized, was deeply informed by Cecchetti ballet technique. As Corvino matured as a teacher, he realized that Laban and Cecchetti had a great deal in common.

Corvino pointed out that the basics of the Cecchetti system were influenced by the earlier work of the Italian choreographer and teacher Carlo Blasis (1797–1878), in terms of movement dynamics and the positions of the body, which Blasis had inherited from the even earlier French choreographer and teacher Pierre Beauchamps (1631–1705).

Blasis was interested in the shapes made in space by a dancer's body, rather than the geometric floor patterns stressed by the teachers of Beauchamps's era. Blasis had looked to Leonardo da Vinci—as exemplified in his famous diagrammatic "Vitruvian Man" drawing—for a scientific explanation of the principles of the body's equilibrium in movement. He related the physical laws of equilibrium to an understanding of balance, placement, alignment, and turn-out. He also analyzed different body types and explained how they resulted in different individual movement styles. Blasis's book *The Code of Terpsichore*, published in 1828, stressed the importance to the dancer training process of harmonious lines that he named (e.g., perpendicular or horizontal). His codification of classical ballet, or the *danse d'école*, was the basis for much nineteenth-century European ballet instruction.

Cecchetti studied in Italy with Giovanni Lepri, Blasis's prize pupil. Corvino may have learned about Blasis in his training sessions with Margaret Craske. He almost certainly learned of the codification of Cecchetti's method in the 1922 book *A Manual of the Theory and Practice of Classical Theatrical Dancing*, by Cyril W. Beaumont.

Corvino felt all these ideas were similar to Laban's theory of the body operating within the structure of the icosahedron, the twenty-faceted, three-dimensional, platonic solid formed by connecting the vertices of the three planes that bisect the body. He pointed out that the basic Cecchetti *port de bras* positions correspond to the Laban spatial scaffolding, and both Cecchetti technique and Laban-based techniques such as Jooss's are concerned with the use of diagonals (although in Cecchetti technique the lower body is not aligned along the diagonal pathways).

Because he was able to go down to the floor, as in modern dance, and up in the air, for ballet, Corvino felt very comfortable moving within the icosahedron's spatial framework. He also believed that these principles, whether specified or not, were essential in the training of a dancer. In looking at a photograph of his daughter Ernesta, Corvino said, "To explain that further, you really need the Laban icosahedron," meaning that the balancing energy lines of the body running through the arms, legs, torso, and head were aimed toward very definite points in the icosahedron.

For Laban, it was essential that dancers be able to know and use their bodies and discover the relationship between the body, its immediate surrounding reach space, or kinesphere, and the larger space of the studio or stage. In addition, Laban, like Jooss and Corvino after him, believed it important to understand and work with whatever body the mover possesses.

Laban's concept of dynamics—Flow, Weight, Time, and Space—was contained in Jooss's choreography and in the company classes, which also included spatial concepts such as the diagonals and spatial relationships. They were not necessarily named specifically, since Laban's theories were not discussed in Jooss's technique classes, but they were part of the combinations and were sometimes discussed afterward. Company classes combined these concepts with ballet. The directness and simplicity of Jooss's choreography, with its sure feeling and definite purpose, remained with Corvino forever.

When he later studied Labanotation—Laban's symbol system for recording movement in written form—Corvino felt it was like ballet because where the body goes in space and where the arms are at any given point in time are precise and essential to both. To Corvino, the emotion or the quality of a movement was congruent with the timing of the movement and its path through three-dimensional space. In a general sense, this is true in Labanotation as well.

When asked whether he used Dalcroze or Laban theories in teaching ballet, Corvino's answer was, "They're there in the ballet; they don't belong to it." From his point of view, most teachers and dancers simply do not take the time to pull them out. The qualities are in *pliés*, in walking, and in the timing of movements. Are you going to lift the leg quickly and bring it down slowly, or the opposite? Done one way it will elevate, and then come down again, in a natural movement. Done another, the emphasis is on the control against gravity.

From Vilzak, who came from the French school and had studied with Nikolai Legat, Corvino learned to sharpen his focus and to make further use of his athleticism. Regarding the seven small notebooks he filled with Vilzak's combinations, Corvino said he wished to understand the "complications" of the classes, in which the actual exercises were short and quick. He regarded the writing down of these combinations as a memory exercise that taught him to think.

Corvino was also very influenced by the classes he took with Margaret Craske and Antony Tudor, even though they came late in his training. From Craske, he took the idea of the plumb line, even more musicality, a sound anatomical approach, and the codification of the Cecchetti technique. From Tudor came an emphasis on expression and the idea that movements must be meaningful, a concept Corvino emphasized in his teaching at Juilliard. He also found much in common between Jooss and Tudor—the use of gesture and the belief that you do not superimpose an emotion on a movement; rather, the emotion arises from and is a result of the movement. What is important, therefore, is a sureness and clarity in which movement is expressive rather than showy.

Corvino said he had read a book about the Cecchetti technique, probably Beaumont's, and then realized that much of it had been employed in Pouyanne's classes. When he began teaching at the Met, Craske had him take the special workshops she gave in the Cecchetti syllabus. Cecchetti had entrusted Craske with the job of disseminating his specific approach to ballet. The Cecchetti method involves a set of exercises, different for each day of the week, which includes all the movements in classical ballet (as codified by Blasis), as well as Cecchetti's additions to the *port de bras* exercises. The material ranges from basic exercises at the *barre* to more elaborate adagio and allegro combinations in the center. Intended for professional dancers, it stresses and develops rhythm, line, and expressivity.

As usual, Corvino looked, listened, and absorbed, and since it all made sense to him, he simply incorporated it into his teaching. When Tudor brought him to Juilliard, where Craske and Martha Hill were adamant that the ballet technique be pure Cecchetti, he took the copy of the syllabus Tudor gave him and followed it exactly, but he also added his own ideas and exercises.

It was the combination of all these elements, influences, and events in Corvino's life, as he perceived and digested them, that led to his own ideas of what dance really is and how ballet should be taught.

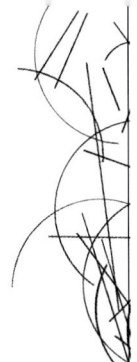
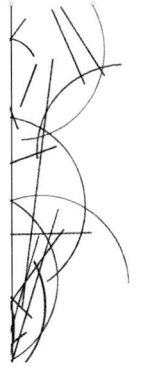

Chapter 9

THE CORVINO
APPROACH

A ndra and Ernesta Corvino both teach what the latter calls "our approach to classical ballet technique." This is based on their father's basic tenets, acquired from their years of studying with him and Margaret Craske, teaching together in the same venues, and countless discussions. The information that follows is drawn from lengthy meetings with Alfredo Corvino, with his daughters, and with the three of them together. Irene Dowd's overdrawings on the photographs are the result of her presence at many of these explorations and actual demonstrations. She also studied with Corvino when she was a student at Juilliard.[2]

Teaching the Grammar, Science, and Logic of Dance

Corvino never deviated from his conviction that a teacher imparts information by demonstration and that the student learns everything through the experience of actually doing a movement. He felt that everyone has the ability to reproduce what he or she sees, but some are more resistant to doing this than are others. To Corvino, ballet was like grammar: the student first learns the words, then phrases, then sentences, until finally, the reason for the grammatical structure becomes clear. "It's not that I want you to do it this way, it's just the way it is," was Corvino's comment to many students.

2 Descriptions of the exercises at the *barre* and the Seven Movements provided courtesy of Ernesta Corvino.

To Corvino, the concept of a "good" movement is one that works. "Either you land properly so you can move into the next step, or you miss it." In his mind, he taught "classical dance" that was unmannered, musical, and stressed sound body placement. And since it was not a style in itself, it could be applied to any dance genre or style because it was based on harmony. He asked for clarity, calmness, the expenditure of only the necessary amount of energy, and the willingness to think.

Since Corvino believed that there was a science at work in dance, just as there is in motors, he would sometimes demonstrate the principles of physics using props such as a fork, a top, a stick, or a spring. In this way, students developed their ability to see the basic principles of movement at work and to think about how those principles related to their own body movements. He was also very definite about the fact that a movement creates its own musicality. Here, his favorite example was Charlie Chaplin in his silent films, implying that the comedian's meticulously planned movements created a rhythm that could be seen, although not heard.

Corvino felt there are two elements necessary to make a dancer: teaching and training, which also includes drilling. By his definition, teaching is sharing a movement and the particular way of performing it, using demonstration and imagery. Training is asking the student to emulate and perform this movement over a period of time, in conjunction with other movements, until it is understood intellectually and physically and belongs to the student's mind and body. To Corvino, this was education by means of a series of logical connections, and it resulted in dance. Drilling is the repetition of a step or short phrase over and over. When it is finally absorbed, it is a single element, like getting a ball in a basket, but it is not dance. To him, properly taught minds and properly trained bodies require a minimum of drilling, which, when substituted for teaching, only solidifies errors and produces tension and weakness.

Corvino's overall approach for beginners, as well as for advanced professionals, was based on the concept of a pyramid, with balance as the base, leading upward to coordination and flexibility in the middle, and resulting in strength at the top; all of these elements must be supported by musicality. Andra points out that this progression derives from a

European model for sports training, and Corvino must have developed it through his own involvement in sports.

Corvino's strong feelings about musicality in relation to the pyramid were expressed in a statement he handed out at a workshop for teachers in 1979:

> *Rhythm and musicality must be carefully nurtured in the class-room, if a young dancer is to attain full growth as a mature artist. The following of the beat must be taken further and lead to the extraction of the musical line through contrasts in the phrasing of the movements. Shading the impulse of the movements in conjunction with the quality of the music creates a dynamic sense, which, when well integrated, allows the muscles to respond correctly to the given movement. The involuntary response of the muscles is virtually impossible to control on the conscious manipulative level ... Therefore; the success of the quality of movement and muscular development of the dancer depends on the musical responses learned by the body. This must start from the instant the dancer begins training and is not something that can be learned after the positions and basic shapes are taught.*

The Seven Basic Principles

Because of his exposure to so many different approaches to dance and his method of working them out in his own body, Alfredo Corvino came to espouse seven principles that he felt governed ballet: stance, turn-out, placement, balance, rules of classical technique, transfer of weight, and coordination. These principles give each student an equal opportunity to develop and progress within his or her own body capac-ities. He and his students felt these principles were as applicable to modern dance as they were to ballet, which is why so many modern dancers studied with him.

Basic stance is the physical balance of all the parts of the body in relation to the plumb line or vertical dimension and comes from the placement of the head in relation to the spine. Corvino believed that aligning the body in a natural and harmonious relationship to that line creates mental and spiritual balance as well. To arrive at one's basic stance, the dancer, standing in first position, focuses his or her attention inward, senses his or her body weight, and allows the feet to connect with the floor. Then, with support from the back, he or she lengthens the body forward and up from the head, thus shifting his or her weight toward the balls of the feet. If the dancer has achieved correct alignment in this process, he or she will then be ready to move in any direction. Correct alignment is what results when one part of the body is balanced in relation to another, for example shoulders over hips.

Turn-out is a cylindrical outward rotation of the limbs. It must be approached as a direction of energy that is integrated throughout the body, not just by isolated muscular focus. In the lower body, it is achieved by bringing the heels forward while turning the thigh bones outward in the hip sockets. This results in opening the front of the hips and engaging the upper thigh and gluteal muscles. The principle of turn-out applies to the upper body as well as the lower. In the arms, the outward rotation of the heels of the hands in relation to the upper arm bones encourages a release of the muscles of the shoulder girdle, allowing the shoulder blades to find their natural placement on the back.

Placement is the relationship of body parts to each other and has to do with alignment and body stance. It is what each individual does to achieve the correct alignment and the ultimate ease of working with his or her body. To Corvino, this related to the use of arms, legs, hands, and feet, as well as the torso. There is no strain or gripping to achieve proper placement. "You don't make your body fit ballet, you allow ballet to fit your body," Corvino often said. His most frequent example of how to achieve proper placement was to hold a stick gently at one end with his fingertips and allow it to hang. After dangling and swaying slightly for a second or two, the stick eventually comes to hang plumb with gravity, having found its own proper placement without strain.

Balance is the equipoise between two contrasting or opposing elements. In ballet, it exists in both movement and stillness. Corvino used the *arabesque* as an example of the body in balance. In an *arabesque*, the curves of the spine deepen, the head shifts forward and up, and the gesturing leg rises to the back, creating one long curving shape, like a comet with a tail. The supporting hip joint is a fulcrum for the "dish" of the pelvis, as it, too, tilts appropriately to create the long graceful curve of the *arabesque*. The arms are placed strategically to equalize the shape. The forward stretching arm and the backward stretching leg are two opposing forces. The standing leg provides the solid relationship to gravity, to which the gesturing leg and both arms relate as the whole body creates the balance of the *arabesque*.

The rules of classic technique in ballet can be traced back to the underlying concepts of classicism in art, as seen in Greek and Roman sculpture, where naturalness, simplicity, and lack of distortion are key. From its beginning in Renaissance court spectacles through its codification by Carlos Blasis in the nineteenth century, ballet has evolved techniques for the use of the body, in stillness and movement, in order to embody those classical values.

The five positions of the feet and arms (e.g., first, second, third, etc.) and the eight directions of the body (e.g. *croisé*, *effacé*, *écarté*, etc.) orient the body in space. The outward rotation of the limbs; stretching of the legs and feet; use of *épaulement*, or positioning the shoulders, neck, and head in relation to the legs and feet; and the soft roundness of the arms are all physical attributes required to create the balance and harmony that are hallmarks of classical ballet. The concepts of traveling *en avant* (forward) and *en arrière* (backward), and of revolving *en dehors* (outward, away from the supporting leg) and *en dedans* (inward, toward the supporting leg), offer a technical structure to create balance as the body moves through space.

Correctly executing specific movements—such as proper *port de bras*, or carriage of the arms, where the hands lead the movement of the arms as they draw arcs in space, rather than an angular arm movement initiated by the elbows or shoulders—may also be considered a rule of classic technique. A dancer must learn each of these very particular ways of coordinating the body in order to achieve the naturalness, simplicity, and grace of classical ballet.

Learning about the transfer of weight—which is where Corvino felt dancing really *happens*—begins by placing the weight on one or two legs and then shifting it. He would first ask, "Where does the weight come from?" Then he would try to lead a student to find and use his or her own weight to initiate a shift in space, pointing to its source in the center of the body. The head and limbs are involved in the change of weight because both are capable of either aiding the process or throwing it off balance.

The ability to transfer weight quickly and with ease in any direction is the main element of coordination, one that Corvino felt required a great deal of concentrated thinking before it could become an instinctive part of moving. He used a *grand jeté* as an example, noting that many young dancers think of it as a split in the air. However, it is really an arc through space. To perform it correctly, the dancer has to push off the back leg, taking his or her center of weight with him or her through the air, and land gently on the front leg as the weight shifts quickly and easily through the front foot.

Coordination is the relationship of one moving part to another. Corvino felt musicality plays a strong role here. To Corvino, much good dancing is a result of properly visualizing movement. The phrasing of a movement, which is aided by this visualization, makes it easier to do. For instance, spotting—the quick whipping action of the head used to achieve multiple turns—is a learned rhythmical coordination that can be achieved by visualization and phrasing.

The *Barre*

The exercises at the *barre* are an opportunity to "ground" the body. Corvino compared the process to plugging in an appliance. Only by "plugging in," or attending to his or her individual body mechanics in relation to the spatial and musical patterns of the movements, will a dancer find the "electricity" or energy for the more difficult exercises in the center. These exercises increase range of motion in the joints, develop an awareness of timing, and improve the dancer's line. The range of motion is increased gradually and without strain by emphasizing dynamics and line.

The proper use of the *barre* begins with placing the hand on it, elbow slightly bent and slightly in front of the waist. The body is approximately one foot away from the *barre*. The hand, palm facing downward, is resting, not gripping, and the thumb is relaxed. Use of the *barre* involves equal opposition in two ways. The hand at the *barre* presses gently downward as the body lifts up. This lever effect lengthens and strengthens the supporting side. Equal opposition also exists between the supporting side and the gesturing or working side, as the hand at the *barre* is also connected horizontally to the opposite shoulder, and the pressure from the supporting hand gives the whole shoulder girdle freedom to expand.

Attending to space is also an important focus of the exercises at the *barre*. Corvino spoke of space as an invisible partner. He said, "The first time I stood in first position, it changed my life. It was an opening into space and life."

The following is a brief description of the Corvino *barre* as described by him and his daughters, and as observed by watching him teach. Most of the exercises end with a balance on *relevé*. Sometimes the given position is established on *relevé* before the dancer takes the hand off the *barre*. Often the dancer must rise after taking the hand off the *barre*, creating the leverage to rise within the body itself, and using the counter-tensions of the invisible partner, space. Sometimes there are dynamic balances that involve transitioning from one position to another while maintaining the *relevé*.

In between exercises, the dancer is given time to practice and absorb what is being discussed so that he or she can work deeply, both physically and mentally. Constant improvement is the result of getting to know one's body through the understanding and application of the work.

1. *Opening and Pliés*

A Corvino ballet class begins with the dancer standing at the *barre* in first position with fingertips on the shoulders. The dancer is given time to feel placed and grounded by lifting the heels slightly off the ground.

This low *relevé* is achieved by taking the head forward and up. With the weight on the balls of the feet, the focus is on lengthening the alignment of the body in relation to the vertical plumb line, feeling one's cylindrical rotation from the core of the body outward, and expanding and deepening the base of the shoulder blades by rotating the upper arms slightly outward. From here, the dancer extends the arms forward and then to second position and slowly lowers them to *bras bas*, while lowering the heels and turning the head away from the *barre*. At this time, the first *plié* exercise commences.

The opening *plié* combination consists of *demi-pliés* and *grand pliés* in first and second positions only, along with *port cambré* forward, back, and sideways. (*Grand pliés* in fifth position are done midway through the *barre*, as part of either the *rond de jambe* or *fondu* sequence when the dancer is warmer. This is because *grand pliés* put more stress on the hips and knees than do *pliés* in first and second position, in which the legs descend evenly from the hips.) Fourth position *grand pliés* are done only rarely because they are extremely stressful for the hips and knees.

Rather than being an exercise for the legs, the *plié* is approached as a practice to lower and lift the torso with proper *aplomb* and timing for both adagio and allegro work. The Corvino class stresses the importance of coming up from the *grand plié* in one continuous movement without stopping at the *demi-plié* level. In fact, the recovery from all *pliés* should be slightly quicker than the descent because the dancer is learning to work with gravity. This trains the body for proper jumps and *relevés*.

The *cambré* forward is done as a stretching/lengthening exercise rather than a strengthening one. The spine is neither stretched completely nor rolled through, either during the lowering of the torso or the recovery. Instead, it is a gentle folding and unfolding at the hip joint, with the torso in one long and internally supported piece. The *cambré* back is initiated by lifting the head and encouraging it to lead the spine up and over in an arc, so that the dancer is supported throughout the spine and does not "break" at either the neck or the lower back. This trains the body for a proper *arabesque*, where the torso and raised leg should make a half-circle rather than an L shape.

2. *Demi-Plié with Passé Retiré*

The second exercise at the *barre* is devoted to working on the placement and energy of the *passé retiré*, with the working foot placed to the side of the supporting knee. *Passé retiré* is done at this point in the *barre*, after *pliés* in first and second positions, as the hips and knees are already flexed and supple. It is done from first position to the side of the knee to maintain the evenness of the hips. A well-stretched and lifted *passé* is important for setting the leg in preparation for unfolding into *développé* and getting maximum pull-up through the dancer's center to aid in balance and engage the muscles of the back, and to aid in getting the dancer centered and supported for jumps, turns, and balances in the *passé* position.

The Corvino approach emphasizes the difference among the three *passé* positions—front, side, and back. *Passé* to the side of the knee is often referred to as *passé* in the neutral position, as it corresponds to first position of the feet. It is also the highest *passé* a dancer can do. *Passé* to the front or back of the knee, called *passé* or *retiré devant* or *derrière* respectively, is used mostly for turning, jumping, and *relevé en pointe*.

But whether front, back, or at the side of the knee, the working leg must be drawn up with a free hip, and it must rotate outward like a cylinder, with the heel and the calf coming forward so that the knee goes back naturally. The *passé* should never be pressed back. Care should be taken to counter-rotate outward evenly on the supporting side, while lifting the head forward and up over the supporting leg.

Even though this is only the second exercise at the *barre*, it is a very challenging one, as the ending requires a low-pressure *relevé*, without the help of the *barre*. The result is the strengthening of the connection between the muscles of the core and spine with the muscles of the inside of the supporting leg.

3. *Tendu*

A Corvino *tendu* combination emphasizes the proper alignment of the pointed foot in all directions, with the heel forward at all times;

the proper quality of *plié*, whether the *plié* has a melting quality or a rebounding quality; and the ease and suppleness of both the pointing and unpointing of the foot. The dancer is encouraged to approach the opening of the foot in one direct movement, without breaking at the metatarsal joints or "dragging" them on the floor. Pressing the meta-tarsal heads on the ground produces stiffness in the foot and leg that can lead to injury. The foot must be trained during the *tendu* and *dégagé* the same way it will be used in jumping. Corvino often said that the *tendu* was about a push and pull, and that it came from the torso and the back.

4. Foot Stretch Exercise

This exercise includes an articulation that isolates the thrust of the toes off the floor. It is not meant to be confused with either *tendu* or *dégagé*. The first four counts begin in first position. Flexing one foot and knee, the dancer shifts his or her weight to the ball of that foot, then, in a quick thrust, points the toes off the floor. The dancer then gently returns the ball of the foot to the floor, and finally returns the heel down to first position. The exercise can also include the quick pointing of the foot in one movement, as well as other movement elements. The foot stretch can also be done from fifth position with changes through *cou-de-pied*, simulating *changements*. As with all Corvino exercises, there are limitless possibilities as to the content and sequence of a given combination, as long as the basic principles of timing and placement are observed.

5. Dégagé

The *barre* progresses with a *dégagé* combination that may include allegro *développé* at 45 degrees and/or 90 degrees, transfers of weight via *coupé* or *tombé*, or any other number of movements that prepare one for allegro movement. Most often the *dégagés* are given in one movement, with the accent inward and a natural rebound outward. However, *dégagés* in two movements, one out and one in, may be given. These train speed and strength into the leg by requiring a quick and held thrust outward and a strong, solid finish in the closed position.

6. *Rond de Jambe*

The *rond de jambe* exercise may include, in addition to basic *rond de jambe a terre* both *en dehors* and *en dedans*, *rond de jambe* slightly off the ground, *rond de jambe* in two movements, *développés*, *demi* or *grand rond de jambe*, *battement enveloppé*, or various combinations of *port de bras* coordinations. The end of the *rond de jambe* sequence may include one or more of the following: *grand plié* (often in fifth position), *port cambré*, *renversé*, lunges for stretching the *arabesque*, or even turns at the *barre*.

7. *Fondu*

The main function of the *fondu* exercise is to train the dancer to raise and lower the body, via the head, in a slow, fluid adagio manner. Corvino often demonstrated this principle by lowering and lifting a small chain. As he held the top of the chain, the dancer could see each link following the preceding link, whether it was collapsing on the way down or straightening into line again on the way up.

From *relevé*, the supporting ankle relaxes first, enabling the heel to lower. After the heel lowers—not before—the knee bends. On the way up to *relevé*, the first thing to lift is the head. The rest of the body follows in sequence—spine, pelvis, thigh, knee, and, finally, the heel. This enables proper alignment through the supporting knee and greater efficiency in movement.

8. *Frappé*

Frappé is one of the keys to good jumping. It is practiced from the *cou-de-pied* position, with the working foot wrapped around the neck or ankle of the supporting foot. The action of the *frappé* is a strike, not a brush. The timing is such that the thigh and knee engage, lengthening at the same moment that the foot points—not after. This is done quickly but gently, so as not to injure the knee or ball of the foot.

When the foot returns to the *cou-de-pied*, it "unpoints" rather than flexes. Flexion makes the leg too tight, slows down the ability to beat quickly, and puts the wrong emphasis on the movement musically. Corvino likened the strike of a *frappé* to the punch of a boxer.

9. *Petit Battement*

The *petit battement* exercise is for the direction and timing of *batterie*, or beating. Even though it is executed with one foot at a time and a flexed knee, the dancer learns how to move the foot sideways out and in, rather than forward and back. Although the foot will alternate closing between front and back, the primary action of the lower leg hinging from the knee is sideways. In a Corvino class, *petit battement* is sometimes executed with a fully stretched foot and sometimes with a relaxed foot, where the ball of the foot stays in contact with the floor. On occasion, it is also given with a wrapped foot *sur le cou-de-pied*.

Corvino often mentioned that he would practice *petit battement* "by the clock," the way a boxer practices with a punching bag. The movement should vibrate like the beating of bird's wings. The lower legs should bounce off one another with "sideways *ballon*," and the action should be reflexive and not "muscled."

10. *Grand Battement*

The *grand battement* exercise is given at a tempo that allows the leg its natural release at the top of the movement. The practice of moving the limbs via the extremities really comes into play here. Corvino would say, "Do the movement from the foot, and the leg will follow." The same goes for the hands and the arms.

The foot brushes on the floor as the dancer creates a "pulley effect" by pressing down on the *barre*. This makes the *battement* very powerful and increases the speed of the foot's escape velocity at the moment the foot leaves the floor.

11. *Stretches at the Barre*

The *barre* concludes with stretches, where the leg is resting upon the *barre*, first *à la seconde* and then *à la quatrième devant*. This exercise finishes with a *grand rond de jambe en dehors*, a *penché* in *arabesque*, and a balance in *arabesque en relevé*. More complicated variations, including turns and shifts of weight, are added as the student advances.

The Seven Movements

In addition to adhering to the seven principles, Corvino also adopted the seven basic movements, as passed down in the technique of ballet known as the *danse d'école*, or French style, that he learned from Pouyanne. This list helps to organize the basic movement qualities that occur in all dance. It can be remembered by the anagram P.E.R.G.S.E.T., and it is translated from the French as:

Plier—to bend

Étendre—to stretch

Relever—to rise

Glisser—to glide

Sauter—to jump

Élancer—to dart

Tourner—to turn

What follows expounds upon these movements, as well as some additional movement qualities that can be considered subsets of the initial seven.

Within *plier*, there exist two different qualities, a melting one and a rebounding one. *Fondu* may be considered a subset of *plier*, as it has a melting quality. *Pliés* that use a rebound may be considered to have *ballon* and will be used for certain jumps, *relevé*, and recoveries.

Étendre is the quality of stretching, which actually applies to all ballet movements. Even a *plié* or a *retiré* has to be stretched. The direction of energy is always extended, even when the muscles contract.

Relever can be accomplished with either a pressure or a spring. *Relevé* can also have a variety of levels, which are more about height than quality but are worth mentioning:

quarter (low), **half** (medium), **three-quarter** (high), and **full pointe**.

Corvino said that the quality of gliding, or *glisser*, is an illusion and that a proper *glissade* is one of the most difficult steps to master because it is not a jump or a drag. Instead, it is composed of *tendus*, which are what allow the body to glide. For example, in a *glissade* to the side, the dancer starts in fifth position. One foot brushes low off the floor, extending the leg to the side, while, simultaneously, the other leg bends. The dancer then separates from the floor, extending both legs and feet equally into second position in the air. There is a transfer of weight as the dancer lands in *plié*, on the foot that first brushed against the floor, while the other leg remains extended low to the side, in a mirror image of the take-off. The dancer then closes the extended leg in fifth position *plié*.

Within *sauter* ("to hop" in French), lies a quality particular to ballet known as *batterie*, or beating. Beating is done mostly with jumps but can also be done *á terre*, or on the ground, with one foot, as in *petit battement*. The quality of *ballon*, or bouncing, is also a subset of *sauter*. *Petit allegro* and *grand allegro* are two different qualities of jumping, each requiring different timing and muscular response. Corvino always described jumping as "separating from the floor." He said, "If the rhythm is right, the jumping is very easy." He always pointed out that Leonardo da Vinci observed that when a man jumps, the head travels twice as fast as his feet.

The quality of *élancer*, or darting, is more horizontal than *sauter*. It is quick and direct, like a dart. Certain jumps, for instance some *grand jetés* and some *sissonnes*, are meant to be *élancer* and will completely lose their effect if done with height.

The most important thing to master for balletic turning, or *tourner*, is the head-spot. Corvino said that one must have a feeling for turning, "like riding a bike." If a dancer can balance well on one leg but does not turn well, then the head-spot must be improved. Corvino would often demonstrate the principle of the winding and unwinding of the neck by holding a belt from the top with a heavy buckle at the bottom. He would twist the belt several times, and the student could see how, when released, the belt would not only unwind but actually start to twist in the opposite direction.

In a Corvino class, the dancer is made aware that during a turn, the torso always has an incoming side, regardless of whether the direction is *en dehors* (outward) or *en dedans* (inward). Each side should revolve around the center evenly, and the entire body should have a flipping quality, as though it were flat. Great attention is paid to arm position and the placement and energy of the gesturing foot. The multifunction of the head-spot is discussed and practiced with special exercises. The spot serves many functions, including orienting the dancer in space, balancing the body during the turn, keeping the dancer turning during multiple turns, or, when used in conjunction with the opposition of the outgoing shoulder, stopping the turn.

Six Photos Illustrating the Equipoise of the Corvino Approach to Classical Ballet Technique

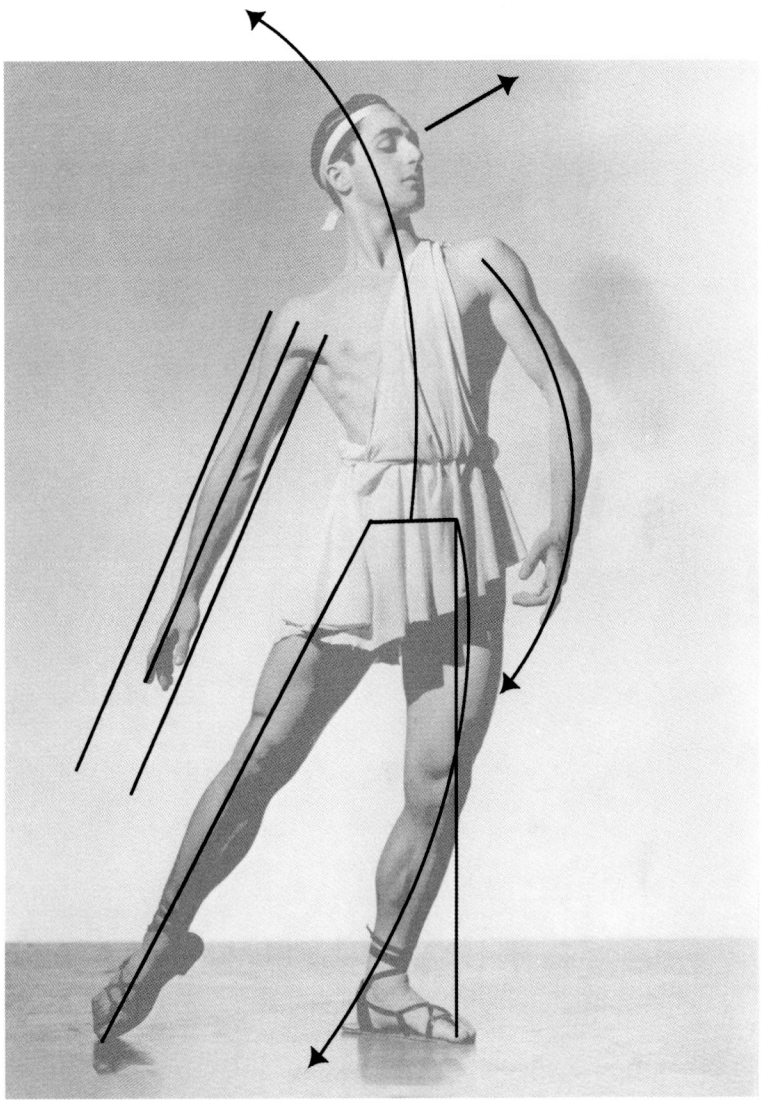

38. The curve of the left arm is reflected in the curve of the left leg and in the curving of the spine, or vertical axis. The line of the right arm is reflected in the line of the right leg. The gaze is at a right angle to the vertical axis. On both arms, the index finger is in line with the shoulder joint and centered between the top and the bottom of the arm pit.

Corvino in Léonide Massine's Seventh Symphony, *circa 1941*

photo © Maurice Seymour, line drawings by Irene Dowd

39. The vertical axis runs from the tip of the toes through the pubic bone, to the top of the spine and center of the skull and out the center of the palm.

Andra Corvino, studio portrait, 1970

photo by Les Carr, photo courtesy of the Corvino archives, line drawings by Irene Dowd

40. The left arm and right leg create a perfectly balanced curve on top of the vertical axis that goes from the foot to the center of the forehead.

Ernesta Corvino as the Sleeper in her ballet Somnus, *1989*

photo by Les Carr, photo courtesy of the Corvino archives, line drawings by Irene Dowd

41. The shoulder blades move down and out as the arms rise, creating a spiraling motion that continues through to the fingers.

Andra Corvino, studio portrait, 1981

photo by Les Carr, photo courtesy of the Corvino archives, line drawings by Irene Dowd

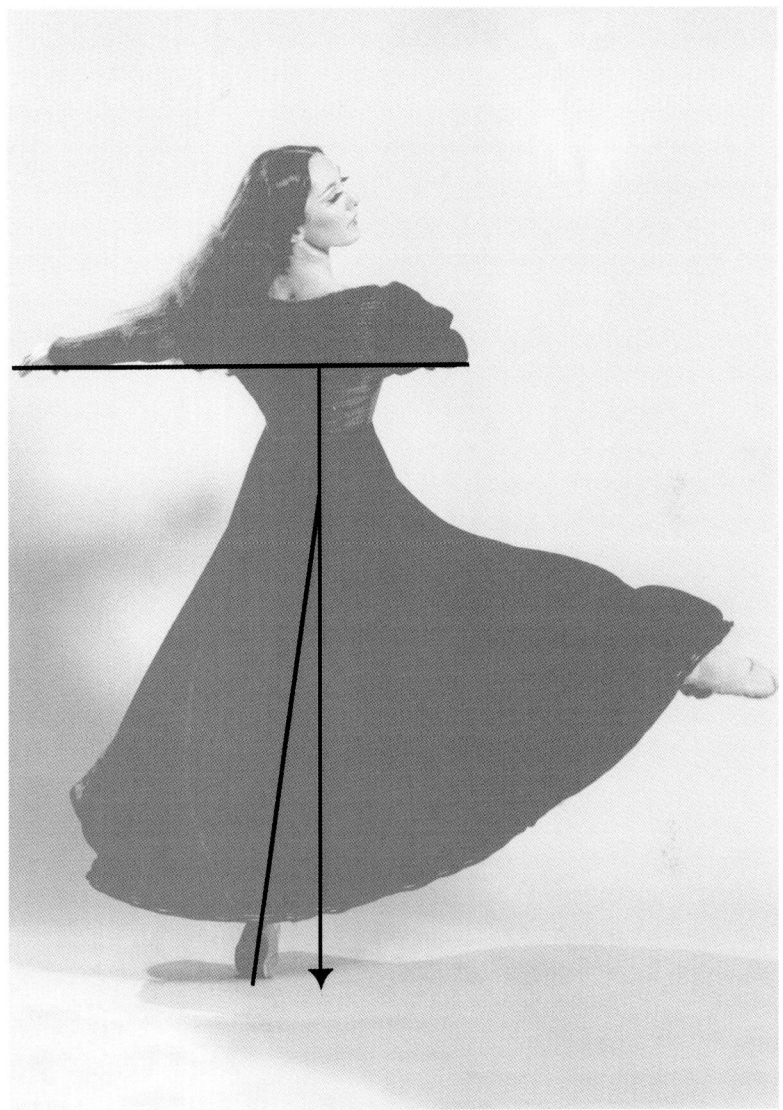

42. The horizontal arms are parallel to the ground and perpendicular to the line of gravity, even though the pelvis is shifted forward in the direction of the right leg.

Andra Corvino as Mona Lisa in Ernesta Corvino's ballet The Gallery, *1981 photo by Les Carr, photo courtesy of the Corvino archives, line drawings by Irene Dowd*

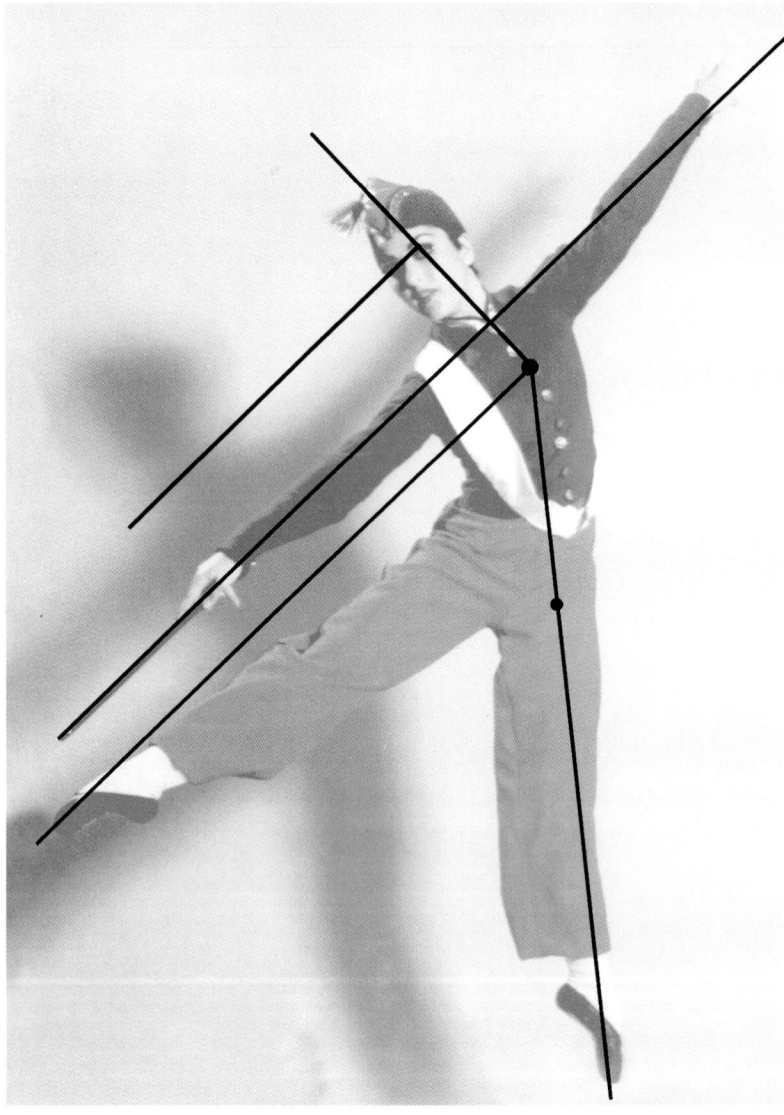

43. In the air, the right arm, leg, and gaze retain their parallel relationship. The line from the center of the chest to the ends of the left toes passes directly through the center of the hip joint.

Ernesta Corvino as the Fifer in her ballet The Gallery, *1981*

photo by Les Carr, photo courtesy of the Corvino archives, line drawings by Irene Dowd

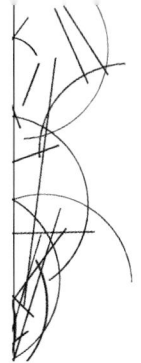

Chapter 10

Corvino's Students
Remember

Over the course of Corvino's many years of teaching, thousands of students spent varying periods of time studying with him. Their reactions and memories are as varied as their careers in dance turned out to be. What follows is a summary of interviews with a cross section of these former pupils. The majority studied at the Met or Juilliard, but some went to Dance Circle as a result of recommendations from other dancers or teachers.

The Whisper Teacher

To take a class with Alfredo Corvino was to enter another atmosphere, to leave behind the pressures of both your personal world and the dance world at large. It was a place where each individual was important, and all were treated equally in a calm, understated, respectful manner. Corvino's comments were positive and rarely critical. He would walk by, look at a student, really see what was happening, and go to the other side of the room to demonstrate a principle, sometimes using a stick or another prop. His aim was to distill the essentials, the universal common denominator in all dance.

In this environment, with his careful oversight and guidance, Corvino's students were able to work steadily and carefully. The sequenced exercises and combinations were usually repeated from day to day, increasing in complexity as the week progressed, often with subtle changes. If you were not paying attention, you missed the changes.

Corvino operated on the assumption that, if given the basic principles in a relaxed manner, the student who wished to learn would take them, think about them, work on them alone, and eventually absorb them. This put a certain amount of responsibility on students, many of whom were young and more readily impressed and motivated by an aggressive, flamboyant teaching style. Some, who needed explicit explanations for every step, took years of study and practice, as well as the gradual acquisition of maturity, to understand, in hindsight, what they had been given.

For others, it took mere months to understand and begin to apply what was being taught, which was basically how to think about change and, hence, movement. Some did not want or were unable to be reached and found class boring. But Corvino did not want someone to make the same mistake over and over. Occasionally, although very rarely, he would ask someone who was not listening to leave.

In his attempt to lead his students to see dance in its totality, in its relationship to life outside the classroom, Corvino used the Socratic method. He asked questions, sometimes tricky ones, and would then, after a reflective pause, give his own answer. This was true communication, for which class time was allowed. It led one to think beyond instructions and rules, to be able "to connect the dots." The query, "How long do you stay in *plié* before an *assemblé*?" is one of those remembered by some of his students. He did the exercise over and over until they discovered for themselves exactly how much time was necessary to go up or come down.

Some called Corvino "the whisper teacher" because of his soft voice and Zen-like approach, but he watched each pupil with a concentrated intensity. He was consistent and fair, with a gentle sense of humor and an endless amount of patience (although one student, recalling the only time she saw him get angry, says it was terrifying). Corvino's sense of humanity and need to communicate flowed forth from him to his students and, eventually, to their audiences.

The joy of working well pervaded the studio, and Corvino's own beautiful physique and demonstrations, described by many as "gorgeous," were as instructive as anything he said. Many remember not his words but what he did; by watching him, you could learn exactly how much energy to put into a movement for one of his soaring and effort-less jumps. In his later years, when he was more physically restricted, he managed to communicate through subtle body movements and the use of his hands to demonstrate.

Corvino offered his students the tools and structure required to build a body for the stage, but at the same time, it was okay if that was not your plan. He looked at the intention inherent in a movement and the success in achieving it. He would often have someone who did not have an ideal body demonstrate a movement, as long as it was evident that he or she understood the principle behind it. For him, you were not presenting yourself, you were presenting the movement. He tried to share an understanding of how the body wants to move as a whole, coordinated unit.

A Rigorous Simplicity

Class was basic but not as simple as it seemed; only now do so many of Corvino's former students realize that his class was solidly packed with material and deceptively difficult. Irene Clark, who started studying with Corvino when she was fourteen and performed with the Dance Circle Company, says he trained her to dance forever. She also recalls that he was fond of saying that something may be simple, but that does not mean it is easy.

The class was composed of tightly organized units in which one section led to the next, a journey of action and energy. On successive days, Corvino would rearrange the modules, with the same material combined in different ways. The pace was even, with a consistent thread running throughout. For example, a class beginning with the *demi-plié* would continue to focus on the *plié* throughout the lesson. The lack of complexity in the structure of the phrases allowed students to add two plus two plus two. When the phrases and technique they required became more complicated, students felt they had a secure base on which to build and proceeded to go through class with a con-fidence gained from each particular lesson and those that had preceded it. This helped them develop trust in their teacher and, even more important, in themselves.

The *barre* always took forty to forty-five minutes, and after a while, the body knew it and could respond. Starting in first position at the *barre*—with the fingertips resting on the shoulders while allowing the body weight to settle down through the legs in a series of little bounces—automatically settled the body and the mind, focusing them both and preparing them gently for all that was to follow. Toward the end of the *barre*, there were always *pirouette* turns that ended with one leg extended *à la seconde* or in *arabesque*, in order to emphasize the need to stay lifted and to reiterate the relationship of balance to weight, since the former was impossible without a keen awareness of the latter.

Jumping was taught as a separation from the downward pull of gravity, creating for the audience a sense of weightlessness. Corvino would say that the people in the balcony could see the top of a dancer's head. Hence, a lengthy time in the air was essential in order to make them fully aware of this victory over the force of gravity, and the dancer had to think of extending him- or herself through the top of the head. Adagio, on the other hand, had to do with allowing the body to fill the space with designs and depended upon the life-giving breath underpinning it.

After adagio and small jumps came traveling across the floor, often ending in an *attitude* or *arabesque* balance. Since Corvino defined all movement in terms of motion—stillness was never static—here he stressed flow and the importance of direction in relation to the body. In *piqué en avant*, he asked the dancer to discover how far he or she traveled to arrive over his or her leg.

Lessons Learned

Certain things remain vivid for all of his students in regard to what Corvino taught. First, there was natural alignment, neither rigid nor aristocratic. Correct placement was necessary so that there was no stress, and the alignment had to be maintained during a change of weight, through sensitive and careful attention to the changing relationships of one part of the skeleton to another. It was this that allowed dancers to adapt what they learned in his classes to other techniques, and one of the reasons so many modern dancers took his classes.

The focus on the *plié* was never forgotten by anyone who took class with Corvino. He referred to it as "a dancer's best friend." Many students remembered him saying that it was essential to breathe into a *plié* or to know how much time you spent in fourth position *plié* before a *pirouette*.

Timing was the underpinning of Corvino's approach. To him, it was what gave quality to a movement. Everyone felt that the importance of timing was learned from the very first *pliés* and *port de bras* exercises. If you learned the correct timing for each movement—a *pirouette*, for example—you could improve and develop an ability to do multiple turns. If you disregarded the timing, it quickly became clear that it was virtually impossible to advance. It was through timing that one learned to appreciate the richness and interconnectedness of ballet technique as Corvino taught it. For example, he stressed that *tendu* and *fondu*, timed properly, are the preparations for jumping and that many actions, for instance the *dégagé* and *demi-plié* at the beginning of an *assemblé*, must take place in exactly the same time frame so that the whole body assembles in the air simultaneously to create that weightless moment of flight.

Musicality was a factor mentioned by all of Corvino's students. Classes were often complicated rhythmically, but with few distractions thanks to the simplicity of the combinations, the rhythm always became clear. There was a dynamic relationship between movement and music. Dancing off the musical beat, which Corvino related to the heartbeat, was not tolerated.

Corvino is remembered for his imagery and analogies. One dancer remembered him saying, "A *penché* is like a spoon balancing on your finger—it needs equilibrium." Another recalled him saying, "To turn, you have to ease your mind," implying the image of emptying the mind, which related for that student to the Zen concept of meditation.

Corvino also used imagery and analogies to cultivate jumping and allegro. He talked about a bird becoming skinny as it went up and plump as it came down in order to encourage the dancers to spread their body weight through their entire frame if they were landing in an extended shape, such as an *arabesque*.

Energy and how a dancer uses it were discussed constantly. Corvino felt that energy determines the quality and form of a step and is as important in stillness as in movement. He said that most young dancers used too much energy and that it was important to learn the minimum amount needed for a particular step. One student recalled that once, while teaching *ronde de jambe en l'air*, Corvino spoke of a moon shot that had recently been aborted, explaining that it would have taken too much energy for the spacecraft to reverse, so instead it had to continue on course and orbit around the moon in order to gain enough centrifugal energy to slingshot back home. It was the same with the *ronde de jambe*—to make the most efficient use of energy, it had to follow the curve.

Finally, everyone commented on Corvino's development of beautiful feet. He stressed the importance of the floor and the fact that the placement of the foot on the floor determined the success of an action. His instruction was always, "Caress the floor."

Corvino's Influence on Teachers

Of the many who studied with Corvino, countless teachers emerged before, during, and after their careers onstage, and most of them are still teaching. They teach ballet, modern, jazz, stage combat, and choreography to children, adults, and professionals. Toni Lacativa Farkas, who danced with Helen Tamiris and Norman Walker, as well as the Dance Circle Company, and has taught adults and children (especially the latter), summarized what many others expressed: "To Corvino, teaching was not about transferring information, but about trust in the teacher/student partnership." When she realized what education really is, thanks to him, she was able to take his ideas and principles, without frills, and share them with her students.

Corvino's idea that his students would learn best if he quietly demonstrated a movement and then left them alone to master it themselves worked well with some but left others completely baffled. Richard Lyle Thomas says this teaching method helped him figure things out before he began to teach himself. He originally taught at Dance Circle and then went on to the New Dance Group. Tina Curran was frustrated and afraid to ask questions during her Juilliard days, and as a result she tries to vary her own approach in order to reach all her students. Now, however, she understands what was being passed on to her, and she goes back to Corvino's simple exercises—the ones that incorporate sound movement principles—in her teaching at Interlochen Arts Academy. The principles she learned from Corvino also influence her efforts to train teachers to apply the Language of Dance method, based on Laban's ideas, when working with young children.

The concept that the foot has to be as sensitized as the hand in expressiveness and suppleness has remained with Anthony Salatino and Peter Sparling, with the latter incorporating all the images Corvino used from nature. Salatino was a ballet major at Juilliard and danced with the New York City Opera, with Ballet Brio, and in Europe, before establishing his own company in Syracuse, New York. Sparling danced with the José Limón and Martha Graham companies and teaches at the University of Michigan, where he has his own company. For Judith Chazin-Bennahum, who performed with the Joffrey Ballet and the Met Ballet, it is Corvino's thoughts on *épaulement* and the relationship between the torso and the line of the foot that lingers. After ten years of teaching, she also began to duplicate his quiet focus. Also a dance historian, she eventually became the chair of the Department of Theater and Dance at the University of New Mexico.

The attempt to draw out students by means of positive energy and to help them grow as individuals, especially if they are young, is a Corvino lesson many of his students-turned-teachers have adapted. They appreciated the safe and relaxed atmosphere of Corvino's classroom. Ellen Kogan, who now works with children with disabilities, tries to share Corvino's belief that one can have the power to control one's own body and overcome disabilities in an attempt to go beyond what seems possible. Rebecca Lazier, a more recent Corvino student who is now a choreographer as well as a performer, was led by Corvino to ask herself how you give students the ability to re-create a movement for themselves. For Stephen Pier, who danced with the Limón company, the Hamburg Ballet, and the Royal Danish Ballet, and is currently on the faculty of Juilliard, his experience with Corvino has everything to do with how he teaches, especially his use of language. For example, Pier might ask his students, "What does *assemblé* really mean?" incorporating the Socratic approach of his former teacher. Nancy Scattergood Jordon incorporates everything she learned from Corvino into her many jobs as a rehearsal director who has staged works for Michael Uthoff, Daniel Lewis, and Lila York, among others, and has worked with Juilliard students. Gay Delanghe, who danced in Lucas Hoving's company, wrote down all of Corvino's coaching prompts and, when she began to teach advanced students at the University of Michigan, used his entire theoretical approach in modern and ballet.

Some of Corvino's students incorporate his approach alongside that of other teachers or apply it to other specific techniques. Ahuva Anbury, a Juilliard graduate, teaches mostly Graham technique in the United States and Israel but has also incorporated the Corvino basics, especially the carriage and use of the arms. She also cites the influence of Craske and Tudor.

Others mention that Craske's, Tudor's, and Corvino's approaches were complementary, with flow being an important element to all of them. The English choreographer Richard Alston, who studied with both Corvino and Cunningham, teaches a Cunningham-based warm-up to his Alston Dance Company (based in London) but feels there is a commonality between the Cunningham and Corvino techniques. Before forming his company, Alston danced for Ballet Rambert, where he made use of the classical technique that he learned from Corvino.

Antonia Franceschi, who starred in the film *Fame* and subsequently danced with the New York City Ballet, presently teaches Alston's company. The two met in a class at Dance Circle. Carla Maxwell, the longtime artistic director of the Limón company and a Juilliard graduate, retains the fundamental movement principles that she learned from Corvino in teaching Limón technique. She finds some similarity between Corvino and Nanette Charisse, who also influenced her, because both offered a broad, nourishing, holistic base.

Joyce Herring, who was a principal dancer with the Martha Graham Company from 1981 to 1994 and, at one time, director of the Martha Graham School in New York, observes that Graham and Corvino said the same thing, emphasizing the essence or truth of the movement. According to Herring, Corvino helped her do what Graham wanted her to do. In her own classes, she teaches all of his basic fundamentals. In May and June 2005, she invited Corvino to teach class for the Pascal Rioult Company for which she is currently associate artistic director, prior to their performances at the Joyce Theater. It was to be the last time that Corvino taught.

Corvino's Effect on Performance

Those dancers who took class with Corvino during or just prior to the beginning of their professional lives felt that he enabled them to extend their time onstage. He gave them ease and fluidity, teaching them how to use just the right amount of energy to control and perform each movement. It was Corvino's emphasis on musicality that allowed the body to do this. Their *plié*, for instance, acquired a pleasurable depth and became more accessible on stage. Some found that after being in his class for a while, they stopped developing cramps in performance. For this reason, many took his early evening class before going to the theater, often already wearing stage makeup. Others would come daily before rehearsals.

Corvino's classes gave his students the tools necessary to figure out and absorb different combinations and to be able to differentiate between technique and style. They responded with less resistance to and anxiety about learning new works and performing them. Many found his approach to be romantic, and as a result, their stage dancing became more lyrical.

The ability to experience movement in a relaxed manner allowed many students to work through or bypass a problem after being hurt.

Whether in school or a company, they always sought out Corvino's classes after an injury.

Comparing Teaching Methods

When asked to compare Corvino's classes with those taught by others, his students most often mention Craske and Tudor. This is not surprising since so many of Corvino's students studied with them as well, and they were the greatest influence on the refinement of his own approach.

Janet Panetta, who has served as ballet mistress for Pina Bausch's Tanztheater Wuppertal and has her own studio in New York, characterizes Craske as the technician, Tudor as the intellectual, and Corvino as the spirit-raiser and confidence-giver. For all three, everything had to come from the inside, but Corvino was the one with whom you could have fun. He was the one who allowed and encouraged the idea of dancing within the Cecchetti-based technique, considered by some to be a dry, overly technical approach to ballet. It was noted by many that while taking class with Tudor, one felt oneself to be in the presence of a great man, but you could go from receiving praise to brutal humiliation in a single session, a traumatic swing for which you had to be thoroughly prepared beforehand. However, taking class with Corvino, particularly before a performance, was like being in what Judith Chazin-Bennahum called "a warm bath."

Toni Lacativa Farkas observes that there are really two ways to teach ballet: (1) begin with the positions, followed by the understanding, or (2) start with the quality of movement, and then go to the positions. It was the latter approach that Corvino took, and very few others joined him in this.

To his students, Alfredo Corvino was really able to be an American teacher, a quality Chazin-Bennahum sees him as sharing with Robert Joffrey. He could go beyond the *danse d'école* and prepare you for a life in dance. Somehow, he was part of the ethics of the fifties and sixties. He was interested in modern dance, understood jazz, and was able to recognize that there are many different ways of moving in America, all of equal value.

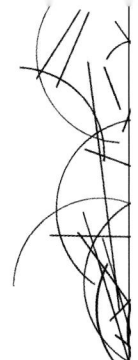
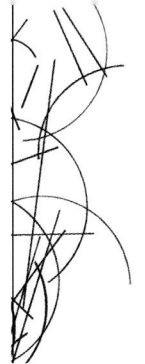

Chapter 11

RETURN TO MONTEVIDEO: COMPLETING THE CIRCLE

When Alfredo Corvino left Montevideo in 1940, he expected to be gone for six months. He did not return for thirty-one years. As he explained, he came to New York, got into the Ballet Russe, and was then drafted. He planned to take Marcella back to Uruguay after they were married, but Andra was born, he was working constantly, and then Ernesta arrived. The developments of life and work were nonstop.

Corvino finally brought his mother and sister to New York for a visit in 1969, after he, Marcella, and the children had moved to Manhattan. The more than twenty-year gap since he had last seen them did not, at the time or later, seem so extraordinary to him. He had kept in touch by mail and telephone, and continued to do so always. Marcella said that he had the capacity to live from minute to minute, without regret or second-guessing himself, and that she had never known anyone so capable of doing so. "His attitude is 'We'll deal with it when it comes.' That's the way he has lived his whole life, and I've learned to live it with him."

Homecomings and Hurt Feelings

In thinking back, Corvino said he had never thought about coming to the United States. Because he knew some French, and Pouyanne had studied in Paris, that was a place to which he imagined immigrating. Buenos Aires was also an attractive city. The Teatro Colón hosted all of the famous choreographers, dancers, and companies, and had a company of its own. Many of the good dancers from Montevideo went there, and Corvino said his next step would have been to go as well because the company at the theater was, technically and in terms of repertory, on a higher level than any in Montevideo.

In 1971, when Corvino returned to Uruguay for the first time, he found it had not changed much, and he enjoyed seeing family and old friends. The dance community, some of whose members felt deserted by Corvino, was not always welcoming. His sister had joined the Friends of the Ballet in an attempt to keep him informed, and she wrote him frequently to that end. From the time of that first visit, Corvino returned roughly every two years. He taught only once on these trips. That was the time before his final visit, and the class was held at the Ateneo, where Pouyanne had first taught him.

Corvino remained in contact with Pouyanne for a time after he left Montevideo, but when it became obvious he was not returning to Uruguay, the communication, for all intents and purposes, ceased. Corvino did inform him of his marriage, and Pouyanne's response was a letter saying that if they lived to see their twenty-fifth anniversary together, then he would send congratulations. Marcella felt this represented the end of a friendship, but she also pointed out that Corvino was Pouyanne's "baby," and his former teacher and mentor had put a great deal into him, both personally and professionally. Hence, she thought Pouyanne probably felt not only disappointment but also a sense of betrayal. When Corvino left to join the Ballets Jooss, he had been the young star, was starting to teach and choreograph, and might have become the core of what Pouyanne envisioned as an especially remarkable development of ballet in Uruguay. Ironically, it was Pouyanne who encouraged Corvino to audition for the Jooss company.

Hometown Press

Among Corvino's memorabilia are press clippings that he either brought back or were sent to him from Uruguay. One, from 1954, about the drain of dancers from Uruguay to other countries, says that one way to solve the problem might be to invite someone like Corvino to come back as a guest. Another, headlined "Alfredo Corvino Took Himself Away for a Month 22 Years Ago," is not dated but, since it mentions the ages of his daughters, was probably from 1962. Basically a piece expressing great pride in their compatriot (as did all subsequent press coverage), it quotes Corvino's mother and sister as saying that every year they receive a letter informing them he has too much work to come home and that it would be easier to bring them to the United States.

In February 1971, the newspaper *El Diario* published a photo and short article entitled "From the Auditorio to the Metropolitan," which summarized Corvino's dance career. In 1978, the same newspaper reported that each evening Corvino spent in Montevideo, he was meeting with local luminaries in the dance and music world in a dance studio, smiling with a modest and serene air, and remembering all he owed to his country and Pouyanne.

On March 28, 1978, *El Diario* published a feature interview entitled "Alfred Corvino: Uruguayan Who Triumphed in New York." Describing him as a disciple of Pouyanne who also triumphed abroad via his merits, it summarizes Corvino's dancing, choreography, and teaching, mentioning Marcella and the girls. The interview ends with its subject saying he is happy to be visiting his country and to be able to help his compatriots in New York. One understands the reference to the "suave wrestler/fighter" in the article because it is signed "Humberto Dolce," who had become a well-known journalist. It is accompanied by a photograph of Alfredo— with his cousin Humberto, cigarette in mouth, in the background. Another article in the newspaper, dated Sunday, March 26, 1978, was headlined "Alfredo Corvino: A Visit from New York." It stated (incorrectly) that this was his first visit in thirty-six years but otherwise summarized his life, teaching, and family details fairly accurately.

Sinfónica, a Uruguayan magazine devoted to the arts, published an article in January 2000 about the appearance of Corvino in Montevideo, again summarizing his career and reporting that he had been invited to attend a rehearsal at the Auditorio.

An Unbroken Circle

Corvino's last trip to Montevideo was in January 2005, when he received a call from his cousin Alberto Dolce (the youngest son of Carlos), telling him that his sister had fallen and suffered a slight concussion. Margarita had never married, had retired from her job as a secretary, and was living in the apartment her brother had bought for her and their mother. When she was diagnosed as suffering from a form of Alzheimer's, she was moved to a nursing home, and the apartment was rented. Alberto and his wife became her guardians, with the help of their daughter Mónica, an accountant. Corvino sent money whenever it was needed and spoke to them frequently by telephone.

Corvino stayed with his cousin a week longer than he had originally planned, enjoying the company of his relatives and meetings with some of his old friends, as well as Liliana, an architect and the granddaughter of Graviel Corvino. Humberto Dolce had died some years earlier. One of the people he saw was Olga Banegas, with whom he had danced in Pouyanne's company. She gave him some programs and photographs of their time together.

As Corvino approached his eighty-ninth birthday, he seemed to be allowing himself to become nostalgic. As was his wont, he never expressed regret about leaving Uruguay, yet one wonders what he thought or felt about his former teacher and his former home. As a teacher himself, he knew the work entailed in the training that had been lavished upon him. Yet, there is no indication that he saw Pouyanne prior to his teacher's death in 1971 or that they were even in contact. He never again had a friend like his cousin Humberto. He missed the climate of Montevideo, and he could never think in English the way he did in Spanish.

Corvino loved Pina Bausch's company and its dancers, and they loved him in return. Philosophically, one could view this last working segment of his life as the completion of a circle or part of the ever-expanding confluence of events and people that gave balance to his life and work.

Alfredo Corvino died on August 2, 2005, in the intensive care unit of St. Luke's-Roosevelt Hospital in New York City. Andra and Ernesta were with him. For weeks the waiting room of the hospital unit had been filled from early in the morning to late in the day with a constant rotation of friends. There was a spontaneous gathering that filled the house on West 50th Street as soon as the sad news was spread. It enveloped the garden and kitchen and round dining table with shared memories, keeping the circle initiated by this remarkable man close and on an equilibrium.

BIBLIOGRAPHY

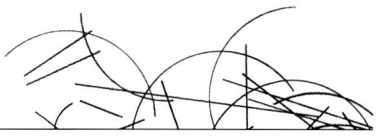

The Corvino archives. In the possession of Andra and Ernesta Corvino, New York City, NY.

The Jerome Robbins Dance Collection, New York Public Library for the Performing Arts, New York City, NY.

The Juilliard School Archives, New York City, NY.

The Metropolitan Opera Archives, New York City, NY.

Salgado, Susana. *The Teatro Solís: 150 Years of Opera, Concert, and Ballet in Montevideo*. Middletown, CT: Wesleyan University Press, 2003.

INTERVIEWS

Interviews and discussion with the Corvinos—Alfredo, Marcella, Andra, and Ernesta—took place over a two- or three-year period. In some instances they were recorded. The tapes are in the Corvino archives.

Akika, Samir, May 29, 2005.

Alfaro, Nancy, July 28, 2005.

Alston, Richard, October 28, 2005.

Anbury, Ahuva, March 1, 2005.

Chazin-Bennahum, Judith, July 24, 2005.

Clark, Irene, October 2005.

Colbert, Margot Mink, May 15, 2005.

Curran, Tina, May 12, 2005.

De Langhe, Gay, February 2, 2005. Via e-mail.

Ellington, Mercedes, May 27, 2005.

Evans, June, April 2005.

Farkas, Alex, July 26, 2005.

Farkas, Toni Lacativa, July 25, 2005.

Franklin, Frederic, March 15, 2005.

Herring, Joyce, April 20, 2005.

Hoge, Beth, February 3, 2005.

Jordan, Nancy Scattergood, June 9, 2005.

Kogan, Ellen, April 28, 2005.

Lazier, Rebecca, May 7, 2005.

Maxwell, Carla, May 30, 2005.

Mercy, Dominque, December 15, 2005.

Mesavage, Ruth, Fall 1998.

Panetta, Janet, December 18, 2005.

Pier, Stephen, January 26, 2005.

Salatino, Anthony, May 6, 2005.

Shimin, Tonia, June 8, 2005.

Sparling, Peter, July 16, 2005.

Thomas, Richard, April 25, 2005.

Wesley, Marguerite, February 5, 2005.

INDEX

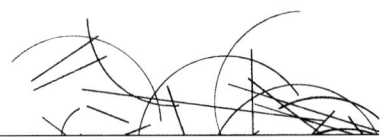